KU-679-418

GANGSTERS

From Little Caesar to The Godfather

The Pictorial Treasury of Film Stars

GANGSTERS
From Little Caesar to The Godfather

by
JOHN GABREE

General Editor: TED SENNETT

GALAHAD BOOKS · NEW YORK CITY

This book is dedicated to Paul Paksarian.

Copyright © 1973 by Pyramid Communications, Inc. All rights reserved. No part of this book may be reproduced or transmitted in any form or by any means, including photocopying, recording or by any information storage and retrieval system, without permission in writing from the Publisher, except for brief quotes used by reviewers for publication in a newspaper or magazine.

Library of Congress Catalog Card Number: 74-33233
ISBN: 0-88365-290-0

Published by arrangement with Pyramid Communications, Inc.

Manufactured in the United States of America

ACKNOWLEDGMENTS

I wish to thank everyone who has given me a hand, accompanied me to the pictures, or discussed movies with me, including Rick Hertzberg, Leonore Fleischer, John Stickney, Natasha Tubelskaya, E.R. Lendler, Bonnie Lee Dry, Jeff Greenfield, Mel Shestack, Bonnie Garner, Jorge Salazar, Mayer Vishner, Dave Warren, Debbie Dozier, Marshall Fallwell, Joel Mason, Jeanna Carroll, and Faye Levine; Bob Somma, Bob Singer, and Gay Bryant for letting me write about films; Ted Sennett, the editor of this series, for surviving; and Andy Bergman, Wendy Holmes, and Jean Vallely for being especially helpful.

The editor wishes to thank Jerry Vermilye and Movie Star News for the photographs.

CONTENTS

This book is based on a pattern of movie-going that is fairly typical for film fans under thirty. Having not had the opportunity to see much more than the last decade and a half of film history at first hand, our sense of the past is dictated by what turns up on television and by what our elders who run the critical establishment have decided are the classics: the movies that show at art houses or institutions like the Museum of Modern Art. This means that our movie-viewing may be as random as that of older fans or that we have a very distorted view based on the pretensions built into film festivals, programs, etc. On the other hand, if a film is truly great, it probably doesn't matter if you saw it at a neighborhood theatre in 1942 or at the Brattle Theatre in 1962, except of course for the

INTRODUCTION

very different point of view brought by each of those audiences. What follows, in any case, are some ideas on the genre set down in the last few weeks of spring 1973 by a devoted movie fan. It is hoped that it will be useful to other fans in finding or remembering movies they want to see among the great many available to them.

The term "gangster film" needs some explaining. The pure gangster film had such a short life, two or three years at the beginning of the 1930s, that a book limited to this period would be focusing on an incredibly narrow piece of film history. What's more, because it would not encompass the films influenced by the classic gangsters, it would severely distort that history. The truth is that the film vocabulary established by the gangsters has affected much of what Hollywood has produced in the ensuing forty years. (For that matter, it has also influenced European motion pictures nearly as much, though only two or three films made in Europe are discussed in this volume.)

Instead, for the purposes of this study, the category "gangster film" has been broadened to include those films about organized criminal activity and those that have been deeply influenced by gangster film iconography. There are limitations on both these categories: organized criminal activity that better suits the definition of "caper," that is, non-criminals and criminals who come together for one job with the emphasis on mechanics, has not been paid much attention; nor have pictures that have come out of Hollywood's penchant for mixing genres—no gangster-horror, gangster-musical, gangster-comedy, and so on. In addition, there are simple limitations of space. Although most of the major films in the genre are mentioned, every reader, and the author, too, for that matter, will find that some favorite gangster film is missing from the text. All that can be said is that a book including every crime film would be encyclopedic.

The most useful aspect of a discussion of genre is that it helps, like the auteur theory, to impose some order on the vast and chaotic history of film. Since it is a mass art, cinema offers no easy distinctions between those works that are certifiably serious art and those that are entertainment. Although in some ways it would be easier to deal with films individually—in the long run this is the only sound way to judge movies—there have been far too many in far too short a period and the opportunities for intense study are too few for careful analysis to have been made of more than a few. There are major filmmakers like Allan Dwan or Joseph H. Lewis, the broad lines of whose careers are obscured, let alone whose individual masterpieces have been analyzed and appreciated. Genre is one way of drawing an outline in which a few tentative evaluations can be made.

Trying to evaluate all films is a task that would overcome all but the most intemperate movie addict, but genre subdivisions begin to make the job manageable. Each genre has its share of successes and failures and it is possible within a genre to begin to work out an acceptable aesthetic, although the latter question is not the purpose of this book. All we are doing here is trying to suggest approximate boundaries and some of the more significant bits of topology on the gangster landscape.

Once you get into a genre you find yourself impatient with its broadness; you discover that you don't want to move on to *The Phenix City Story* or *The Garment Jungle* but to see *Gun Crazy* or *The Big Heat* again and again until you know and understand them. As a critical tool genre is rather like a bulldozer; eventually, you want to take a scalpel to individual movies. Genres exist because the commercial motive in Hollywood encourages the repetition of formulas that are successful commercially. And the formulas are popular because audiences require accessible and familiar handles to make the entertainment work. Be that as it may, the genres, once established, do make a convenient pattern for analysis.

SCARFACE (1932). Paul Muni as Tony Camonte

The outlaw has always been an attractive figure. From Robin Hood through Frank and Jesse James to Ché Guevara, the romanticism of outlaw life has always been captivating. In a world where few enjoy wealth and fewer power, the outlaw has frequently been a hero, a man who beat the system, who made everyone at the bottom feel better by taking a little bit off the top. Throughout history there has been a fine line between the bandit and the political rebel. Almost every successful revolution of modern times has been led by men who were outlaws one minute, statesmen the next. It is hardly surprising that the outlaw holds such sway over the popular imagination.

But one kind of outlaw doesn't fit this pattern; the modern gangster whose scowling visage and violent ways have, for the last forty years, terrorized and titillated American moviegoers. Robin Hood is hardly the model for a character that has been presented mostly as an egocentric monster. Not that it has been quite that simple, especially in the beginning. On film, the gangster is a paradoxical figure: on the one hand, he embodies unimaginable evil; on the other, he is the American dream come true, the immigrant who makes

CARS, GUNS, AND MOLLS

it by dedication and hard work.

The gangster believes that might makes right. He cares nothing for other people's moralities. He lives by a code, but one drawn so narrowly in his own interest that it doesn't act as a limit on his behavior. His business is crime—bootlegging, gambling, prostitution, drugs. He lets nothing stand in his way. His weapons are anything that will do the job. He lives outside society, preying on it, undermining it; left unchecked he would destroy it.

Politically, the gangster is an anarchist, even though his own institution, the mob, is rigidly authoritarian. Wherever he strikes at society he weakens it, destroys its self-respect, leaves it less able to function and survive. His attitude toward society is reflected in the environment he inhabits: he lives in a world of sirens and gunfire, of dark, menacing streets and threatening shadows. His efforts to "be somebody" are successful only at the expense of other people, and he spares no one to satisfy his drive to power. He is tough, cold-blooded, ruthless, brutal, often unbalanced, always as cunning as he is evil.

But he has that other side. If he is the personification of much that is wrong with America, he is also an expression of American ideals. He achieves many of the goals—power, money, fame, status—that are held out by society as symbols of success. What is he if not the rugged individualist, the aggressive entrepreneur. He vanquishes his enemies, overcomes often incredible odds to come out on top. His energy, dedication, and ingenuity make us admire him, in some films even love him.

The gangster first impressed himself upon the public mind during Prohibition when "everyone" was breaking the law and

LITTLE CAESAR (1930). Edward G. Robinson as Rico

by helping them he was, in a sense, performing a public service. The movies were following the lead of the newspapers which for years had been chronicling the battles of civic authorities against the first lords of crime. Hollywood turned the story into its most rigid and compelling genre.

The first major gangster film was *Little Caesar* (1930), directed by Mervyn LeRoy, a journeyman director who fought Warners' front office to do it. Within a year, the gangster film reached its classic period, with the release of William Wellman's *The Public Enemy* (1931) and Howard Hawks' *Scarface* (1932),

and went immediately into decline. There had been earlier films about crime, of course, but none that could be fairly called gangster movies. There had been, for example, Josef von Sternberg's *Underworld* (1927), perhaps the greatest of the pre-*Little Caesar* crime films. Bull Weed, the principal character, is not a mobster surrounded by deferential henchmen, however, but a simple jewel thief whose primarily criminal associates are a collection of shadowy Dickensian back-streeters. Only at the end, where the shoot-out resembles the finale of *Scarface*, does *Underworld* seem like a classic gangster film, and this probably

UNDERWORLD (1927). With George Bancroft and Evelyn Brent

THE ROARING TWENTIES (1939). James Cagney heads his dapper gang of hoods.

because Ben Hecht wrote both scripts.

There were many other crime films in the twenties, of course, including some that included isolated elements of the gangster film. But *Little Caesar, The Public Enemy,* and *Scarface* together and separately embrace all themes and icons encompassed by the genre. All three examine the rise and fall of a gangster: Rico (Edward G. Robinson), Tom Powers (James Cagney), and Tony Camonte (Paul Muni) are all immigrant Catholics caught, or at least afraid of being caught, in powerlessness and poverty; all three are vulgar and aggressive, and, as Andrew Bergman has written, all three are perverse incarnations of the Horatio Alger hero.° All three

° Andrew Bergman, *We're in the Money,* New York University Press, 1971.

16

die similarly, Rico and Camonte machine-gunned in the street, Tom Powers left dead on his mother's doorstep. The defeat and death of the gangster was the most rigid convention of all, dictated not only by the logic of melodrama but by the political demands of the 1930s.

The elements that make up the gangster film can now be isolated:

Clothes: Clothes are a mark of social standing, and the rising gangster uses them to show off. In *The Public Enemy*, Tom and Matt spend their first paychecks on custom-made clothing, and *Little Caesar*'s Rico and *Scarface*'s Tony Camonte both call attention to their fancy new duds. New clothes are used to win over critical friends, lovers, family, as Tony tries to impress Poppy with his new shirts, "one for every day." Racketeers also like their boys to dress well as proof and reminder of how well they're doing. Sometimes important are other signs of wealth, such as houses, apartments, and furniture—Rico is very involved with his "big house," and after the early 1940s, art buying and collecting take on sinister overtones.

Cars: The automobile, like clothes, is a way the rising mobster demonstrates his success. Tom and Matt can't get over the

THE ST. VALENTINE'S DAY MASSACRE (1967). One use of cars

LITTLE CAESAR (1930). The hold-up on New Year's Eve

fact they own such beautiful "wheels" and Gwen (Jean Harlow) is as impressed by the car when they meet as she is by Tom. Cars are also tools: intimidating to those who must be cowed, and useful for getting to and away from the crime. Eventually, the automobile becomes the symbol of the gangster's uncontrollable power and is used literally as a weapon. (Mannix, television's leading crime-stopper, is attacked by an automobile on virtually every show.) By the fifties, the appearance of a mysterious car is enough to strike terror into a potential victim, even before he has seen who is inside.

Guns: The gangster, especially the gang leader, must be quick to use his gun. It is the ultimate source of his power, over his men and against his rivals and public authority, in committing his crimes. It is also the symbol of his outlawry, the image—the "chopper" in *Scarface*, the squat ugly police .38, the high-powered hunting rifle—of his unbridled power. A gangster's gun is part of him; it is his instrument of self-expression, his way of controlling people and events and of making his dreams come true. The Freudian aspects of a gangster and his gun are obvious: it is his way of asserting his manhood; as we shall see, it is sometimes his only way. The car and the gun are probably the two most powerful icons in the gangster film, at least the two that best express the character of the hoodlum. They come together forcefully many times in films as when Rico machine-guns his frightened driver Tony to death from a passing car. It is cars and guns, blasts and screeching tires, that are used in the quick cuts and montages of crime waves and gang wars.

Telephones: The telephone is the other piece of technology at the service of the gangster. It is one of the ways he gives orders; it ties together his empire and it can be used—in fact, is frequently used—to threaten. It is also the way he gets bad news.

There is a startling scene in *Scarface* involving a phone: Angelo, who doesn't relate to telephones very well anyway, is getting a hard time from someone on the other end of the wire. In frustration, he pulls out his gun to shoot the phone.

The City: In *The Gangster as Tragic Hero*, Robert Warshow wrote: "The gangster is the man of the city, with the city's language and knowledge, with its queer and dishonest skills and its terrible daring, carrying his life in his hands like a placard, like a club . . . for the gangster there is only the city; he must inhabit it in order to personify it: not the real city, but that dangerous and sad city of the imagination which is so much more important,

THE DRAGNET (1928). With Evelyn Brent, George Bancroft, and three telephones

WOMAN TRAP (1929). A typical setting for the gangster film

which is the modern world."
The city serves as both the actual background for the gangster and as a symbol of the desolation that produced him and extension of his brutality. The gangster lives in a world of police sirens and empty streets, seedy rooming houses and cheap hotels, luxury suites and penthouses, bus stations, waterfronts and warehouses, speak-easies, nightclubs, and police precincts. Even when the locales have been moved to places like Florida or Nevada, the hoods are seen as city boys holed up in some hideout, never

as enjoying their freedom from the city's terrors. The gangster lives to die, as Rico and Camonte do, in the streets. He never escapes Warshow's sad city of the imagination.

The Players: It would be hard to overestimate the importance of the faces and personalities of the actors who dominate gangster films in setting off the resonances that make the genre work. Cagney and Robinson established the vocabulary that dominated the crime films of the thirties, just as Bogart would dominate the forties. But even

° Robert Warshow, *The Immediate Experience*, New York, Atheneum, 1970, p. 131.

20

more important, perhaps, were the hoods and gunsels who backed up the leaders, adding their faces to the characterless streets of the city: Ted De Corsia, George Bancroft, Elisha Cook Jr., Charles McGraw, Paul Stewart, Allen Jenkins, Marc Lawrence, Jack Lambert, and Timothy Carey, among the faces that have become part of the scenery. Good actors breathe life into the characters they play; in film, because the illusion of reality is so extreme, they *become* the characters. The characters deepen with each portrayal until Bogart in *High Sierra* or Cagney in *White Heat* or Robinson in *Key Largo* have the depth of the men who have *lived* through previous films. We don't see Cagney as just a middle-aged psychotic in *White Heat*; we remember how he started out with his friend Matt on the streets of Chicago twenty years before.

The Roles: In "The Gangster as Tragic Hero," Robert Warshow argues that "the gangster film is simply one example of the movies' constant tendency to create fixed dramatic patterns that can be repeated indefinitely with a reasonable expectation of profit." But he goes on to add that "this rigidity is not necessarily opposed to the require-

THE AMAZING DR. CLITTERHOUSE (1938). Allen Jenkins (extreme left) watches Maxie Rosenbloom, Claire Trevor, and Humphrey Bogart

LADY SCARFACE (1941). Marc Lawrence, with Judith Anderson

ments of art,"[°] as indeed it is not. Much art, especially popular art, involves the exploration of fairly narrow conventions. We are all aware, for example, of how popular songs become ritual through repeated radio play. Rico, Tom Powers, and Tony Camonte are similar characters. They all began poor and powerless, escape the ghetto by clawing their way savagely up through the mob, and pay for their crimes by violent death. This basic character, rougher and smarter than the thugs around him, is the focus of the genre. Intelligent and ruthless, he is surrounded by others less smart and less tough, who are willing to accept his leadership and protection. He exists in a social milieu made up of cops: crusading, crooked or, mostly, dumb; battling district attorneys and mob mouthpieces; private eyes and other, usually reluctant, heroes; stoolies, newspapermen, gamblers, and bookies; newsies, and poolroom and gym operators. Most important of all are the gangster's women—mothers, ladies, and molls.

Sex: The gangster's oversized ambition and aggressiveness, including his preoccupation with his gun, seem to be a result of confused sexuality. At the least, sexual deviations crop up in most gangster movies. In *Scarface*, for example, Tony

°Robert Warshow, *The Immediate Experience*, p. 129.

has incestuous impulses toward his sister Cesca (Ann Dvorak). When Tony makes a fuss over a man's kissing her, it is clear even to her that Tony treats her as a lover. Their mother suggests nervously: "Tony doesn't love you. To him you're just another girl." But when Tony catches her in an apartment with Rinaldo (George Raft), his closest friend, he kills him. And when Cesca comes to kill Tony in revenge, she ends up by joining him in fighting the police, substituting a communion of violence for the forbidden communion of sex. However, before she can get off a shot, before the consummation, Cesca is killed, and with her Tony's reason for living.

Similarly, if not so overtly, Rico is not "normal" sexually. Little Caesar is probably a homosexual. Rico's closest friend, Joe (Douglas Fairbanks Jr.) becomes a professional dancer. "Dancin' ain't my idea of a man's job," says Rico. "Joe, you're getting to be a sissy." This sounds manly enough, but Rico is really trying to get Joe to come back to him, to give up women, especially his dancing partner. Rico threatens to kill Joe if he keeps dancing, but when he tries he finds that

SCARFACE (1932). With Paul Muni and Ann Dvorak

LITTLE CAESAR (1930). With Edward G. Robinson and Douglas Fairbanks, Jr.

he has gone "soft," that he is unable to pull the trigger: "This is what I get for liking a guy too much." Other scenes suggest Rico's homosexuality: Rico, who doesn't form attachments to women, is very close to Otero, one of his gunmen. In one scene, Otero and Rico are lying suggestively on a bed; in another, Rico cradles the wounded Otero against his cheek. It is interesting that it is only in the gangster film, and not in the Western or in war or sports stories, that Hollywood allows itself to raise the issue of homosexuality that is implicit in men-in-groups.

Related to homosexuality is the hostility to women common to almost all gangster movies. Rico's attitude towards Joe's dancing partner makes it clear how distasteful he finds the idea of getting involved with women. On the other hand, Tom Powers' relationships with women are so dominant as also to be aberrant. In fact, when Tom pushes the grapefruit half into the face of his girlfriend, Kitty (Mae Clarke), he commits one of the most hostile acts directed towards a woman in the history of films. Again, when Tom and Matt are hiding out, the woman taking care of them implies that she and Tom made love while Tom was drunk the night before; Tom is revulsed. Although Tom and Rico's behavior is extreme, it is not unusual. Most gangsters act as if women, or at least the women they can get, are whores, and they offer them no gentleness and no affection.

There are two exceptions to this: ladies, as opposed to "dames," and mothers. Ladies are usually rich and smart and they become the Big Boy's property, adding class in the same way cars or clothes do. (The ladies' motive is usually excitement, although some admit that they couldn't live as well any other way; sometimes when the excitement wears off, they are kept in check by fear.) Often the lady goes with the other accouterments of power when one leader is supplanted by another. Gwen (Jean Harlow) becomes this kind of success symbol for Tom Powers, but he is moving too quickly toward his destiny to enjoy or even accomplish his conquest of her: she stays tantalizingly aloof.

The other side of the gangster's aggressive need to prove his manhood is the succor he receives from his mother (and mother-types). The model is established by Tom Powers whose mother is the battleground between him and his straight-arrow brother Mike. Mothers figure prominently in *Scarface* and *Little Caesar*, too, but only Cagney was capable of the scene played with his head in his mother's lap. Tom's father, in the scene where he beats him for stealing a pair of roller skates, is authority, the Law, righteousness; his mother is love, approval, acceptance.

There is one other aspect of the gangster's personality that calls for further examination, his relationship to the gang. Although mobsters are in league out of self-interest—they can pull bigger jobs, afford better lawyers, and protect themselves more efficiently from police—for

THE PUBLIC ENEMY (1931). James Cagney, Mae Clarke, and a grapefruit

his own protection, the gang leader must have dependable henchmen. At least some part of his cruel and irrational behavior is designed to keep his followers afraid. Also, because he is such a supremely existentialist figure, a creature who acts to live, and one who carries individualism to an irrational extreme, the gangster can have no compassion for members of his gang. He depends on the group for his survival, yet will sacrifice any member of the group without hesitation. The gangster, born in and of the chaos of the city, spreading anarchy by his existence, is also mortally afraid of anarchy. Capone's offer of help to the government in rooting out Communists in the thirties was based on more than just a shrewd judgment about what might help rehabilitate him. It is part of the logic of the gangster's life that he is what he most hates.

The final irony is that the aggressive energy of the gangster

THE PUBLIC ENEMY (1931). With Jean Harlow, Edward Woods, and James Cagney

THE PUBLIC ENEMY (1931). With Edward Woods, James Cagney, and mother Beryl Mercer

can have as its realization only death. As Robert Warshow wrote: "It is true that the gangster's story is also a tragedy . . . but it is a romantic tragedy based on a hero whose defeat springs with almost mechanical inevitability from the outrageous presumption of his demands: the gangster is *bound* to go on until he is killed."°

° Robert Warshaw, *The Immediate Experience*, p. 143.

29

Of all gangsters, the one who has held the longest grip on the imaginations of Americans is "Scarface" Al Capone. Born Alphonso Caponi in Castel Amaro, near Rome, in 1895, Capone came to New York with his family as an infant. Like many ghetto children, he became involved in crime at an early age, and by the time he left for Chicago in 1921, he had already sustained in a bar fight the two parallel scars that earned him his nickname.

In Chicago, he went to work for Johnny Torrio, the city's top gangster, as a strongarm man and killer. In 1925, he eased out Torrio (the boss retired after an assassination attempt) and he was able to run the city unchallenged from 1927 to 1930. The legal efforts of public authorities (the mayor called him "public enemy number one"), the extra and illegal activities of vigilantes (including the "secret six"), even the power of rival gangs, the Irish North Side mob and Roger Touhy's Des Plaines gang, were unavailing against Capone's ruthlessness.

It finally took government agents to stop him. After nailing him for two minor charges, failure to appear as a witness in a murder trial and carrying a concealed weapon, the Internal Revenue Service sent him up for an

CAPONE AND COMPANY THE BIOGRAPHICAL GANGSTER FILMS

eleven-year term for income tax evasion. He was released from prison in 1939, sick in body and mind. He died on January 25, 1947.

The Capone story is compelling. Rags to riches. Power unlimited when he was on top. *Hubris* rewarded with damnation when he fell. Among countless films, plays, and books based on the legend were two of the three greatest movies from the classic period of the gangster film, Howard Hawks' *Scarface* and Mervyn LeRoy's *Little Caesar*. The legend was also worked and reworked by several generations of filmmakers. Of the screen Capones, Paul Muni's *Scarface* is probably the best, but he is challenged by Rod Steiger in Richard Wilson's *Al Capone* (1959). Other prominent Capones have included Wallace Beery in George Hill's brutal *The Secret Six* (1931); Neville Brand in Phil Karlson's *The Scarface Mob* (1962) and Joseph M. Newman's *The George Raft Story* (1961); and Jason Robards Jr. in Roger Corman's overblown *The St. Valentine's Day Massacre* (1967).

A montage of Al Capones and prototypes. Top left: Rod Steiger. Top right: Neville Brand. Bottom left: Edward G. Robinson. Bottom right: Paul Muni. Center: Jason Robards

THE SECRET SIX (1931). With Jean Harlow, Johnny Mack Brown, and Wallace Beery

AL CAPONE (1959). With Nehemiah Persoff and Rod Steiger

The differences between Steiger and Robards are instructive, pointing up the dangers and possibilities inherent in playing gangsters. Steiger, an interesting actor with a tendency to emphasize the more extreme sides of the characters he plays, has plenty of room to explore a psychotic personality in Wilson's gritty film. Robards, in Corman's silly and pretentious production, leaves enough distance between himself and the character for a Brinks truck to pass through. Admittedly he is miscast, possibly because it was felt his echoes of Bogart would add to the atmosphere of the recreation. Yet Bogart could never have been successfully cast as Capone; and had he been, he never would have undermined it, as Robards does. He may have handled the role lazily, but without the smirking and eye-rolling that administer the *coup de grace* to an already half-dead film. Broad playing, even by so excellent an actor as Edward G. Robinson in *Little Caesar*, tends to undermine the force of the gangster tale told straight.

The historical accuracy of gangster (or any but documentary) films is probably not very important. Works of art stand or fall on their own merit. Much of Capone's true story appears in the films, but if Capone had never existed, screenwriters would have had to invent him. As it was he provided them with the St. Valentine's Day Massacre (also in *Scarface* and *Al Capone*) and the rubouts of Diamond Joe Costillo and Legs Diamond. Capone's Johnny Torrio becomes Rico's Vettori in *Little Caesar* and Tony Camonte bumps off Costillo and ousts Johnny Lovo in *Scarface*. Capone's tax case is immortalized in Joseph H. Lewis' *The Undercover Man* (1949). Even the famous scar, probably too outrageous for even Hollywood to have thought of by itself, turns up in movies that are only indirectly inspired by Capone as on Judith Anderson in Frank Woodruff's *Lady Scarface* (1941), or that have nothing to do with him at all as on Barry Sullivan in Gordon Wiles' *The Gangster* (1947), perhaps the best performance of Sullivan's career.

Capone is not the only hood to be honored with repeated biographies, but he is the only one who has been presented fairly straightforwardly by all his chroniclers. Only Neville Brand's somewhat too polished Capone deviates from the portrayal of the gangster as a tough and brutal bully. This is in sharp contrast to criminals like John Dil-

YOU ONLY LIVE ONCE (1937). With Sylvia Sidney and Henry Fonda

linger and Bonnie Parker who were rehabilitated beyond recognition in films based on their exploits. For example, Bonnie Parker and Clyde Barrow were far from the Robin Hoods and star-crossed lovers portrayed by Faye Dunaway and Warren Beatty in Arthur Penn's *Bonnie and Clyde* (1968). Closer to reality, perhaps, was William Witney's *The Bonnie Parker Story* (1958), starring a glittering Dorothy Provine in an exploitation version of the story. Fritz Lang turned the story into *You Only Live Once* (1937), starring Henry Fonda and Sylvia Sydney, one of the great films of the thirties, and Nicholas Ray used Far-

ley Granger and Cathy O'Donnell in *They Live By Night* (1949), to make a fit caper for the forties. The legend was also the basis of one of the best "sleepers" of the forties, Joseph H. Lewis' *Gun Crazy* (1950), a beautifully crafted, subtle, moving, if somewhat poetic evocation of the legend.

More exciting even than Bonnie Parker and Clyde Barrow in the eyes of newspaper readers of the thirties was John Dillinger. A kind of real-life Bogart, tight-lipped, tough, easy with women, Dillinger was the most successful highwayman of the Depression, netting as much as $250,000 in 1934 and 1935. Dillinger was also

YOUNG DILLINGER (1965). Nick Adams as John Dillinger

HIGH SIERRA (1941). With Cornel Wilde, Arthur Kennedy, Humphrey Bogart, Ida Lupino and Alan Curtis

menacing enough (or had the good luck) almost never to have had to resort to his gun during robberies, and he probably never killed anyone before being shot to death himself during an illegal raid on a Chicago movie theater by the FBI in July, 1934. Dillinger was everything an American hero should be: handsome, stylish, generous, intelligent, and resourceful. He was credited, probably apocryphally, with introducing the machine gun, bullet-proof vests, safecracking tools, and getaway cars into criminal activity. One wonders

how criminals escaped previously, but the legend demonstrates how highly he was regarded by the public.

That public was protected from any glorification of Dillinger by Will Hays of the Production Code Authority, but a theater gunfight similar to the one in which the outlaw died was a high point of J. Walter Ruben's *Public Hero No. 1* (1935), part of the G-Man cycle. The only classic to be made from Dillinger material was Raoul Walsh's *High Sierra* (1941), the film that boosted Humphrey Bogart to stardom. Muni, Cagney, Robinson, and George Raft had rejected the role of killer-on-the-run Roy Earle before Bogart, who rarely turned anything down, accepted it. The script, by John Huston and W.R. Burnett, takes as its inspiration Dillinger the man rather than repeating the details of his life. "As Earle," Alan G. Barbour writes, "Bogart was expanding on the criminal characterization he had already mastered in a dozen earlier films, giving it greater depth by adding contrasting elements of warmth and compassion to offset the dominant violence." °Bogart wasn't making Earle up out of whole cloth, however, but successfully capturing pieces of Dillinger's public personality. When Earle is released from prison he seeks out children and woods, just as Dillinger, after his escape from the allegedly escape-proof jail in Crown Point, Indiana, went to visit his father. Dillinger's Robin Hood side is demonstrated in Earle's helping the club-footed Velma (Joan Leslie). And the gunman's affection for women is paralleled in Earle's devotion to sensitive, delicate Marie, played

°Alan G. Barbour, *Humphrey Bogart*, New York, Pyramid Publications, p. 73.

BABY FACE NELSON (1957). Baby Face Nelson (Mickey Rooney, left) in a shoot-out

BLOODY MAMA (1970). Shelley Winters as Ma Barker

by Ida Lupino. Like Dillinger, Earle is hunted mercilessly until, cornered, he accepts his death, samurai-like, at the hands of his pursuers.

Unfortunately, none of the other Dillinger-inspired films comes close to *High Sierra*. It was remade first as a Western by Raoul Walsh (*Colorado Territory*, 1949), and then by Stuart Heisler as the dreadful *I Died A Thousand Times* (1955) with Shelley Winters and Jack Palance in the Lupino and Bogart roles. For the rest, Max Nosseck's *Dillinger* (1945), with Lawrence Tierney, and Terry Morse's *Young Dillinger* (1965), with Nick Adams, barely rate footnotes. However, the portrayal of Dillinger by Leo Gordon in Don Siegel's *Baby Face Nelson* (1957) is intriguingly off-beat until he turns into just another gun.

The most recent *Dillinger* (1973), written and directed by John Milius, is also the most ambitious. The first of a new cycle of criminal biographies promised by American International, *Dillinger* has Warren Oates in the title role with Ben Johnson as Melvin Purvis, the FBI agent who relentlessly hunts him to his death. For a man who made his reputation as a screenwriter—Milius worked on *The Life and Times of Judge Roy Bean* and

Jeremiah Johnson among others— the director has come up with an awkward script relying on both narration and titles, one that plays loose with the facts of Dillinger's life and arguably with the personalities of both the bank robber and the G-man. In the end, despite careful attention to detail in the props and costumes and despite the presence of first-rate character actors like Harry Dean Stanton, Richard Dreyfuss, Geoffrey Lewis and John Ryan, the latest *Dillinger* doesn't work.

Part of the problem, certainly, is that with his attention centered on the *mise en scene* and the special effects, Milius exerts almost no control over the actors Very few directors have figured out how to handle Oates so that he doesn't come across as if he's kidding, and Milius isn't one of them. The director also lets Johnson ham it up shamelessly, allowing him to distract from the violence on which Milius is trying to focus. Even the violence is not especially well handled (cf., Sam Peckinpah) and it is all out of proportion to the rest of the film. There is some point where filmmakers might as well abandon the pretense of plot altogether and just go ahead and make pure violence films the way some already make pure sex films. A "V" rating would be of help to the moviegoer who doesn't want to be bled upon.

Baby Face Nelson was the first of a series of films that included *Al Capone* and *The Bonnie Parker Story*, mostly biographies of Prohibition and Depression hoodlums, that continues into the early 1970s. In this category are Roger Corman's *Machine Gun Kelly* (1958) and *Bloody Mama* (1970), as well as his *St. Valentine's Day Massacre*; Budd Boetticher's *The Rise and Fall of Legs Diamond* (1960); Joseph Pevney's biography of Dutch Schultz, *Portrait of a Mobster* (1961), and Richard Wilson's *Pay or Die* (1960), about the development of organized crime in New York in the late nineteenth century.

With only a few exceptions, the film biography has been a sidelight in the history of the gangster genre. And the successes—from *Scarface* and *Little Caesar* through *High Sierra* to *Bonnie and Clyde* —have for the most part been those films that played loosest with their subjects.

In the period after World War I, the rapid expansion of the economy combined with "do-nothing" politics to define the character of the expanding northern urban areas. In large cities like New York and Chicago, masses of people, mostly immigrants or unsophisticated rural natives, poured in to settle in the slums and ghettos, only to find that existing political and social institutions were inadequate to help them. Bewildered and lost in a world they quite literally didn't make, these new urban residents came easily under the domination of political bosses. By providing simple social services, such as assistance in finding jobs or housing or medical attention, and taking advantage of ignorance (often, of course, simply ignorance of the English language) and naïveté, the bosses created a pattern of civic corruption that provided the context for the growth of mob influence.

The puritan ethic in American public life also resulted repeatedly in legislation designed to protect citizens from their own weaknesses and follies, such as laws against gambling, prostitution, and business on Sunday. The Volstead Act which, from its enactment in 1919 to its repeal in 1933, made it illegal to manufacture or sell alcoholic beverages

THE GANGSTER FILM IN THE THIRTIES

was such a law and led inevitably to the expansion of gang power chronicled in *Scarface* and *The Public Enemy*. After repeal, the interest of racketeers in such areas as labor relations, nation-wide gambling set-ups, and drugs can be seen as an attempt to fill the void left by Prohibition, a void that did not exist before the Volstead Act was passed.

It is an accident of history, not some flaw in their collective character, that has caused Italians to dominate the history of organized crime. Each wave of immigrants—the Irish, the Germans, the Jews—had to start its climb from the bottom of the social ladder. By the time the Italians arrived after 1880, the urban political system was dominated by the Irish who had been in the United States in great numbers since the 1840s and whose assimilation had occurred simultaneously with the rise of the cities. Because of their late arrival, Italians were denied political and social power more completely than any other major ethnic group. It is hardly surprising that many among them, like

SCARFACE (1932). With Paul Muni and George Raft

their predecessors, turned or were driven to crime. (The Irish, after all, were regarded as little better than barbarians for several generations and New York's newspapers around 1900 were filled with indignant stories about Jewish crime waves.) If Italians were buying municipal governments, after all, it was Irishmen who were selling.

It should be pointed out that although the Italians dominated organized crime, they never tried to hold an exclusive on it. There were still Irish mobs as late as the 1930s; if Capone was able to beat the Irish Northsiders, it could be because he was just a little hungrier for success. Even the Italian gangs themselves always contained an important smattering of Jews. And if Italians can claim the greatest gangster in Al Capone, Jews can bid fair for the first in Arnold Rothstein.

In an article on Mervyn LeRoy written in 1933, Dwight MacDonald wrote: "I should not hesitate to call *Little Caesar* the most successful talkie that has yet been made in this country."° MacDonald was saying that for

°Dwight MacDonald, *On Movies*, New York, Berkley Medallion, 1971, p. 125.

LITTLE CAESAR (1930). Rico takes a bullet.

ALIBI (1929). With Regis Toomey and Chester Morris (at right)

BLONDE CRAZY (1931). With Joan Blondell and James Cagney

the first time a movie had been made that used cinematic techniques to capture the essence of "real life." In the dialogue— spare and sharp as an argument, in the cutting—fast and nervous as a city street, *Little Caesar* and the films that immediately followed it are more exciting than what preceded them because they capture more fully the illusion that what the viewer sees is happening. As Ben Hecht wrote about *Underworld* in his autobiography:

> An idea came to me. The thing to do was to skip the heroes and heroines, to write a movie containing only villains and bawds. I would not have to tell any lies then . . .

Hecht was wrong to think that villains would not be seen as heroes, but he couldn't know how ready the Depression would make America to applaud its outlaws. His emphasis on realism, on "simple truth" as he called it, was among the elements that were to make his and other gangster films so compelling.

The simple truth, it would turn out, was a hard pill for some elements of society to swallow. Hollywood, in any case, ever ready to exploit a good thing, followed *Underworld* with a cycle of crime films that in-

cluded a remake by Josef von Sternberg called *The Dragnet* and his *Docks of New York*, both in 1928, and Roland West's *Alibi* and Lewis Milestone's *The Racket* a year later. They lacked, as we have seen, many of the elements that make a proper gangster film. *Alibi,* for example, a neglected classic, is less about criminal activity than it is about the efforts of a bad boy to shield himself from the law by taking advantage of the love of a good girl, although it does include some excellent nightclub footage and a prison scene that uses sound beautifully. But if they weren't gangster movies, they were enough to arouse the ire of the "better" elements who began to organize and agitate against the genre almost before it was born.

The side of the angels was led by one Will Hays, president of the Motion Picture Producers and Distributors of America and formerly Warren Harding's Postmaster General and Republican National Chairman. Hays had been hired by the industry to help "clean up" the suggestive films of the twenties and he responded to the new menace by suggesting that "to overemphasize the gangster's role in American life is undesirable." Half the

*Ben Hecht, *A Child of the Century*, New York, Ballantine, 1970, p. 447.

BLONDIE JOHNSON (1933). With Joan Blondell and Chester Morris

THE SECRET SIX (1932). With Jean Harlow and Lewis Stone

cuts reported by the Chicago censors' board in 1930 and 1931 were for "showing disrespect for law enforcement" and for "glorification of the gangster or outlaw," and one-quarter of the cuts by the New York censors were from gangster movies. Wright Patman, even then a Congressman from Texas, went so far as to try to establish a national board of censors.

There might have seemed reason to be worried. Over fifty gangster pictures were released in the year after the success of *Little Caesar* and in most of them gangsters and policemen were killed in great numbers. It must have seemed to the guardians of public order that a generation of citizens was learning how to kill, steal, and bootleg. Films contributing to the craze included Archie Mayo's *Doorway To Hell* (1930), Roy Del Ruth's *Blonde Crazy* (1931), another Cagney vehicle, and Ray Enright's *Blondie Johnson* (1933).

Panic over the popularity of these films led to the enforcement in 1934 of MPPDA's production code which had been enacted in 1930 in response to the first wave of crime films after *Underworld*. It was obsessed with both the idea and techniques of lawlessness:

(I) **Crime Against The Law.**
These shall never be presented in such a way as to show sympathy with the crime as against law and justice or to inspire others with a desire for imitation.

(1) Murder
  (a) The technique of murder must be presented in a way that will not inspire imitation.
  (b) Brutal killings are not to be presented in detail.
  (c) Revenge in modern times shall not be justified.

(2) Methods of crime should not be explicitly presented
  (a) Theft, robbery, safecracking, and dynamiting of trains, mines, buildings, etc., should not be detailed in method.
  (b) Arson must be subject to the same safeguards.
  (c) The use of firearms should be restricted to essentials.
  (d) Methods of smuggling should not be presented.

CITY STREETS (1931). With Kate Drain Lawson, Gary Cooper, and Sylvia Sidney

Although the emphasis was laid on violence, it is well to remember that there were other reasons why the gangster pictures were feared and resented. One reason frequently cited was that the gangster film encouraged disrespect for the forces of authority. When Tony Camonte struck a match on a policeman's badge, he was demonstrating his contempt for the law. In Rouben Mamoulian's *City Streets* (1931), police were played like heavies. In George Hill's *The Secret Six* (1931), public authority is so powerless that the mob can only be challenged by hooded vigilantes who take the law into their own hands. In *The Public Enemy* the police might as well not exist; the war is between competing gangs, not between the police and the criminals. In *City Streets*, hero Gary Cooper, when asked to push beer, can think of nothing worse to say than "Beer? I'd as soon be a cop as that."

More important, gangster films portrayed bankers, lawyers, businessmen, and public officials and other upholders of the status quo as weak and corrupt. The sniveling brewery owner of *The Public Enemy* is a fair representative of his class, so far as gangster pictures are concerned. At a time when the Depression was already calling into question the credibility of the system, it would not do to have the movies advertising its corruption and decadence.

In any case, the gangster's period of glory was over almost before it began, and not only because of the immense pressure from the likes of the Daughters of the American Revolution and the Knights of Columbus. Perhaps because the themes had been exhausted by the films that dominated the period, perhaps because popular art forms tend toward extreme statements to retain their hold on the attention of the audience, the genre was in decline by 1932, the year *Scarface* was made. In films like William Wellman's *The Hatchet Man* (1932), the concerns of the gangster film are played out to extremes in environments that eschew expressionism for the baroque.

Hollywood found it couldn't get along without the gangster,

THE HATCHET MAN (1932). With Edward G. Robinson, Leslie Fenton, and Loretta Young

however, and in 1935, with William Keighley's *G-Men*, the second cycle began. Since public pressure and the new Legion of Decency prevented the depiction of gangsters as central characters, the attention was shifted to the crime fighter. Cagney and Robinson dominated the new period, bringing to the roles of FBI or narcotics agents all the élan and bravado that had made them so attractive as criminals. (In fact, their behavior on the side of the law was sometimes not very different from their criminal behavior.)

The choice of Cagney to herald the new cycle in *G-Men* was perfect, and Hollywood's army of hacks was quickly taking advantage of it with headlines like "Public Enemy Becomes Soldier of the Law." The *G-Men* screenplay by Seton I. Miller carefully lays the groundwork for the conversion. Cagney's Brick Davis has the same background as Tom Powers, only instead of a Putty Nose to set him on the road to crime, there is a gangster patron to send him to law school

G-MEN (1935). With James Cagney and Robert Armstrong (on the left)

BULLETS OR BALLOTS (1936). With Humphrey Bogart and Joseph King

PUBLIC ENEMY'S WIFE (1936). With Cesar Romero and Margaret Lindsay

so that he can escape the slum and go straight. Even his decision to join the FBI is inspired by street values: he wants to avenge the death of a law school chum who has been murdered in the war against the mob. His new badge in hand, he happily guns down everything that moves.

Similarly, Edward G. Robinson turned Little Caesar inside

out in William Keighley's *Bullets or Ballots* (1936). Beginning at the bottom as he did in the earlier film, this time as a police agent, he works his way up through the gang until he is powerful enough to destroy it. Another variation on a theme was Nick Grinde's *Public Enemy's Wife* (1936), in which Pat O'Brien proved that lawmen could be lovers by wooing the ex-moll (Margaret Lindsay) of gangster Cesar Romero. Shortly after these films, because of the successful anti-mob efforts of prosecutor Thomas Dewey in New York, the G-man and the cop were joined by the district attorney hired in films like Lloyd Bacon's *Racket Busters* (1938) to clean up the city.

Hollywood revived the gangster film with special care during this period, aware perhaps that what they were offering now wasn't so very different from what they were prevented from offering before and trying to forestall criticism before it got started. They tried to sell the idea that they were improving the image of the average flat-

RACKET BUSTERS (1938) With George Brent (pointing finger)

A SLIGHT CASE OF MURDER (1938). With Ruth Donnelly and Edward G. Robinson

foot, but G-men, crusading cops, and special prosecutors are, in the nature of things, a different breed from the man on the beat. In the new cycle most cops were still pictured as plodders: you wouldn't need special cops, after all, if the regular ones were doing their jobs properly.

By the end of the decade, the classic gangster film had softened to the extent that humor and sentiment were heavily laced into the mixture. Cagney and Robinson dropped their vicious manner to turn somberly sacrificial, or merely comical. In *The Roaring Twenties* (1939), Cagney gave up his life to save his former girlfriend's crusading husband. In Lloyd Bacon's hilarious *A Slight Case of Murder* (1938), Robinson was a retired kingpin hood who was forced to resort to some of his old ways to get rid of some unwanted corpses. By 1940, in Bacon's *Brother Orchid* he was a gangster who finally retired to a monastery. Even Humphrey Bogart in Lewis Seiler's *It All Came True* (1940) played a gangster mothered by some lovable old vaudevillians.

In the late thirties, yet another element was added to the basic vocabulary of the gangster film. Until then, it was assumed by gangster films that hoodlums were born and not made. Nowhere, not even in the scenes in *The Public Enemy* where Tom and Matt graduate from petty to grand larceny, is there any statement that social conditions breed crime. The gangster must be killed because there is no hope of rehabilitating him: he is what he is. Beginning with William Wyler's *Dead End* (1937), gangster films began to demonstrate an awareness that broken homes, poverty, maltreatment by parents and institutions, and a generalized criminal environment can breed criminal behavior. Films such as Lewis Seiler's *Crime School* (1938), and Michael Curtiz' *Angels With Dirty Faces* (1938) use many of the motifs of the gangster movie to point up the sources of crime. Their focus was usually juvenile delinquency or prisons, but at the center of most of them was a gangster, Bogart or Cagney, who was similar to the ones who started it all half a decade earlier. *Dead End's* Bogart, a washed-up hoodlum named Baby Face Martin, is the gangster in decline, his power shown to be illusory, his ritualistic posturing presented as hollow.

By the end of the thirties, several strains of the gangster mode were running concurrently. David Howard's *Border*

BROTHER ORCHID (1940). With Ann Sothern and Edward G. Robinson

DEAD END (1937). With Joel McCrea, Humphrey Bogart, and Allen Jenkins

CRIME SCHOOL (1938). With Milburn Stone, Gale Page, and Humphrey Bogart

ANGELS WITH DIRTY FACES (1938). With Pat O'Brien and Ann Sheridan

TIP-OFF GIRLS (1938). Emerging from the truck: Anthony Quinn and Larry (Buster) Crabbe

I AM THE LAW (1938). With Barbara O'Neil, Edward G. Robinson, and John Beal

G-Men (1938) or Louis King's *Tip-Off Girls* (1938) might be showing alongside Ray Enright's *Angels Wash Their Faces* (1939), which blended sociological theory into its roughneck Dead End Kids humor, or Alexander Hall's *I Am the Law* (1938), in which Edward G. Robinson dons the badge (or, hefts the portfolio) of the special prosecutor.

A few years later, Robinson, in Lloyd Bacon's *Larceny, Inc.* (1942) was an aging hood who bought a luggage store for shady purposes but ended up helping the neighborhood merchants. Little Caesar had gone soft, and a new kind of tough guy—the hard-boiled detective—was waiting to take his place.

As far as gangster films are concerned, the thirties ended and the forties began in 1941. Two films were released that year, both starring Humphrey Bogart, that can serve as archetypes for two major strains of the genre: Raoul Walsh's *High Sierra* was the culmination of an attempt by Hollywood to recreate the classic gangster hero of 1931-32, while John Huston's *The Maltese Falcon* was the first in a new mode, the thriller, whose hero, more often than not, was to be a private detective.

Like two other important films by Walsh, *The Roaring Twenties* (1939) and *White Heat* (1949), *High Sierra* depends for a lot of its impact upon a deeply conditioned response on the part of the audience to a number of conventions firmly set in the preceding ten years. Walsh is nearly a perfect director for certain kinds of action films because his fast pacing and his lack of concern with the motivations of his characters allow the iconography, stripped to the bone, to carry his stories swiftly along. Roy Earle cannot escape his destiny—nothing can save him. Bogart's death caps both *High Sierra* and *The Roaring Twenties;* in the latter it is Cagney who kills him, as if somehow the reality he portrays is to die with

THE GUMSHOES AND THE THRILLERS

him. Roy Earle's furious pursuers are making an end to the classic gangster character as surely as they are to the particular bandit they have cornered.

But if one strain of the genre had exhausted itself, another was just beginning. It is no slur on the Bible to say that John Huston is only as good as his material. In *The Maltese Falcon* he had a terrific story, as he himself said, "based on a very good book" by Dashiell Hammett, a book that Huston was astute enough to see was actually a screenplay. It was aided, as all of Huston's best work of the forties was to be, by incredibly good casting: Bogart's Sam Spade is possibly his greatest characterization and, like Mary Astor's Brigid O'Shaughnessy, Sydney Greenstreet's Casper Gutman, Peter Lorre's Joel Cairo, Elisha Cook's gunsel Wilmer, Gladys George's Ivy, Jerome Cowan's Miles Archer, Lee Patrick's Effie and the cops of Ward Bond and Barton MacLane, it belonged in the drab, seedy milieu of Hammett's story.

The Maltese Falcon was the

THE MALTESE FALCON (1941). With Mary Astor, Barton MacLane, and Peter Lorre

THE MALTESE FALCON (1941). With Humphrey Bogart and Mary Astor

THE MALTESE FALCON (1941). With
Elisha Cook, Jr., Sydney Greenstreet,
Humphrey Bogart and Mary Astor

first important thriller. Using most of the same elements as the gangster movie, the thriller focused on another lowlife inhabiting the same shadowy landscape, the private detective. Sometimes the objects of the detective's pursuit were gangsters, but just as often not; in fact, in the same way that it made little difference whether hoods made their living by bootlegging or by robbery, the details of the particular case mattered less than the way the hero conducted himself against the mysterious and threatening forces arrayed against him. The recurring pattern of the reluctant and tattered hero puzzling his way through a dangerous, baffling world, as powerful in its mode as the rags-to-riches-to-death cliché was for gangsters, was established by the almost accidental power of Huston-Bogart collaboration in *The Maltese Falcon* and a similarly fruitful and even more unlikely Bogart-Howard Hawks' success, *The Big Sleep*, five years later.

Like its precursors from *The Public Enemy* on, *The Maltese Falcon* is realistic about such matters as sex, violence, and money. Spade, the hero, for example, puts money a bare second to survival: "You will take, say, one hundred dollars?" says Cairo. "No, I will take, say, two hundred dollars," replies Spade. "We didn't believe your story," he tells Brigid, "we believed your money." Money, in fact, is what moves all the characters; it is what keeps them chasing the falcon.

Death, as Dwight MacDonald pointed out, is just one of those things—to the survivors. Spade brushes aside his secretary's sniffling condolences on the death of Archer with an order to have the lettering on the door repainted to read just SAMUEL SPADE. Even his motive for pursuing Archer's killer is not lofty but matter-of-fact: "If your partner is killed, you're supposed to do something about it."

Sex is just sex. Huston doesn't dwell upon the relationship between Brigid and Spade, no prolonged clinches, no histrionics; it's just there. Near the end, when he is explaining why he will turn her over to the cops for killing Miles, Spade says, "Sure I love you, but that's beside the point." He has to get Archer's killer and since she actually did it she seems like the logical choice. Besides, what would keep her from bumping him off when she got the chance? "I'm not going to play the sucker for anyone."

Spade has one talent, survival, the only one he has ever had time to develop. "I'll have some rotten nights after I've sent you over," he tells the woman he loves, "but that will pass." He is a loner who didn't particularly like his partner, doesn't especially like anyone, and actually enjoys hurting people like Cairo and Wilmer. He is also obsessively anti-homosexual. We have seen that physical deformities and sexual eccentricities were part of the vocabulary of the gangster film from *Scarface* on. In *The Maltese Falcon*, not only are Wilmer, Cairo, and Gutman unusual physically—Gutman, in fact, establishes a whole line of menacing fat men, but there are suggestions, as there have been in earlier films, of homosexuality: Cairo has gardenia-scented calling cards and a shady past with a boy in Istanbul; Gutman, dressed in a kimono, takes Spade's arm and places his hand on Spade's knee. Spade, on the other hand, is reluctant to be touched at all. He thinks women are o.k., apparently, but all of the sexual encounters between him and Brigid have undercurrents of violence.

In some of the films of the late thirties the mobster's neighborhood chum, having become a cop or a priest or a lawyer, was added to show that not everyone who left the poor old neigh-borhood escaped in a stolen car. The thriller introduced a new character who didn't quite steal it and didn't quite earn it; the gumshoe did a lot of borrowing without much collateral, and one of the things he borrowed most was time.

There had been private detectives in movies before, of course, but Nick Charles, Sherlock Holmes, and Charlie Chan had little or nothing to do with the gangster film. What was new and different about *The Maltese Falcon*, besides the iconography, was that the hero, instead of being effete and brainy as well as somewhat removed from the crime he is investigating, was tough, shrewd, and fighting for his own survival. Bogart as Sam Spade and later as Philip Marlowe in *The Big Sleep* is one of the more fortuitous bits of casting in the history of movies. He brings his considerable talent as an actor to bear, of course (at least in *The Maltese Falcon; The Big Sleep* may be more of an energetic application of personality), but so completely do his lumpy face and gravelly voice mirror the world that Hammett and Raymond Chandler have recorded, that the character is established from the opening shot. A sense of how right Bogart is in the role can be gathered by comparing his Marlowe to the others: Dick Powell in Edward Dmytryk's *Murder, My Sweet* (1945), based on *Farewell, My Lovely*; Robert Montgomery directing himself in *Lady In The Lake* (1947); George Montgomery in John Brahm's *The Brasher Doubloon* (1947), based on *The High Window*; James Garner in Paul Bogart's *Marlowe* (1969), based on *The Little Sister*; and Elliott Gould in Robert Altman's disastrous spoof of *The Long Goodbye* (1973). All of these films have their merits, some of them considerable, but only James Garner comes close to as apt a Marlowe as Bogart's, and this no doubt because Garner suits his time as Bogart did his a quarter of a century earlier.

The Big Sleep has received rather more attention than it deserves in some quarters, not enough in others. Lovers of clas-

THE BIG SLEEP (1946). With Humphrey Bogart, Lauren Bacall, and Louis Jean Heydt

THE BIG SLEEP (1946). With Lauren Bacall and Humphrey Bogart

sic film structure are put off by its pasted-together style which does jar with the carefully thought-out films of the thirties, even for that matter with the soundly plotted *Maltese Falcon*. On the other hand, devotees of Howard Hawks have tried to see this rescue job of directing as some sort of triumph. And one hardly knows what to make of Pauline Kael's insistence that *The Big Sleep* "split the seams of the well-constructed Hollywood movie." A bit much to ask of a thrown-together thriller of which, by their own testimony, no one, not the director, not the stars—Bogart and Lauren Bacall, not the screenwriters—Leigh Brackett and William Faulkner, not even Chandler himself, had the slightest idea what was going on.

The one thing certain about *The Big Sleep* is that it was meant as a showcase for the explosive personality team of Bogart and Bacall. If there was much "intent" behind the making of the film, it was to give them a place to play. However, its impact was deepened by the force of Chandler's world view.

Chandler is a confusing storyteller, especially for a mystery writer. He is more concerned with depicting the bleak and lonely Southern California endgame than with dreaming up carefully manipulated story lines. In the long run he has proven to be a much more important writer than Hammett, who was a little too intellectual in his conception and a little too slick in his execution to have a lasting impact on writing as a craft. His five novels are enjoyable and they had an enormous impact within the genre, but they lack the raw, slice-of-life punch of Chandler's stories.

We have already seen that the space inhabited by Sam Spade was confusing and menacing, that nothing that *seemed* real actually was. Brigid O'Shaughnessy is also known as Wonderly and Leblanc; Cairo has a library of passports; Brigid betrays Thursby, Archer, and Spade and is abandoned by Spade; Gutman is willing to let little Wilmer, his protégé, take a fall for him; Gutman constantly praises Spade while trying to do him in. Spade is obsessed with facts because he is allowed so few. But Spade was on granite compared to the quicksand that Philip Marlowe wades through in *The Big Sleep*.

Philip Marlowe is a tough, aging private detective brought to life by Bogart's amazing presence. To paraphrase a later generation of Hollywood flacks, Bogart *is* Marlowe. Marlowe is summoned to the mansion of a General Sternwood to enter upon a case of incredible complexity. He encounters Chandler's whole menagerie of California grotesques—blackmailers, pornographers, nymphomaniacs, drug addicts, murderers. Although Chandler was less overtly political than Hammett, his upperclass people were even more immoral: Sternwood bound to his wheelchair and his pathetically dissolute daughters (Lauren Bacall and Martha Vickers, the latter constantly sucking her thumb) spending rather than living their lives.

We are, once again, in Warshow's city of the night, where sensation rather than fact is all.

THE BIG SLEEP (1946). With Humphrey Bogart and Lauren Bacall

WHITE HEAT (1949). James Cagney as Cody, on "top of the world"

POINT BLANK (1967). Lee Marvin gets rough.

code. And all of this in a Los Angeles that is dark and wet with an endless rain.

Three conventions of the thriller are reinforced by *The Big Sleep:* the threat—with tails, phone calls, beatings—by parties unknown; the mysterious, or in the case of Harry Jones quite straightforward, deaths of those with whom the shamus comes in contact; and the desirable woman, in this case Bacall, who will either rescue or betray the hero.

In *The Big Sleep,* the controlled violence that was an undercurrent of *The Maltese Falcon* erupts: Geiger, Brody, and Mars are killed and Marlowe is twice beaten up. Guns and cars are prominent, the one usually

71

KISS ME DEADLY (1955). With Maxine Cooper, Ralph Meeker, and Wesley Addy

GUNN (1967). With Laura Devon, Craig Stevens, and Helen Traubel

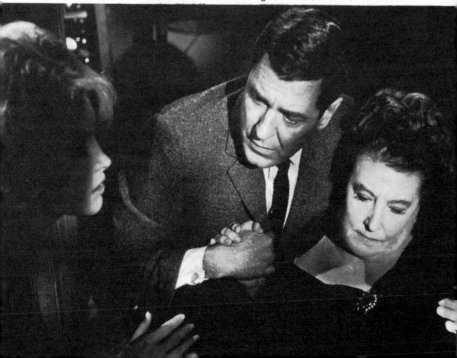

assuring that someone will turn up dead in the other. There are, once again, hints of aberrant sexuality: Carmen's nymphomania, homosexuality between Sternwood and Sean Regan, Geiger's pornography. Sternwood sets the tone right in the beginning as he sits among his orchids discussing his daughters' "corrupt blood." Between them, *The Maltese Falcon* and *The Big Sleep* established conventions as solid and as influential as those set by the classic gangster films. They were reworked many times over in the succeeding decades and probably constitute a more significant part of our movie-going today than does the parent genre.

The forties were the heyday of the thriller, but with some modifications thrillers continue as an important part of filmmaking today, sometimes straight, more often as parodies or low-budget films at the bottom of the double bill. Young directors who were to become famous as genre makers, or sometimes more generally, made first-rate thrillers: Otto Preminger's first important film and one of his few undeniably lasting ones was *Laura* (1944); new directors found the old ones trying to get into the act as Robert Siodmak's *Dark Mirror* (1945) and Phil Karlson's *Dark Alibi* (1946) gave way to

Henry Hathaway's *The Dark Corner* (1946), Delmer Daves' *Dark Passage* (1947), and William Dieterle's *Dark City* (1950). There were countless others: *D.O.A.* (1950), made from one of Siodmak's German films by Rudolph Maté, about a man, Edmond O'Brien, who for no comprehensible reason is dying from a mysterious shot of radiation poisoning; Byron Haskin's gripping *I Walk Alone* (1948); and *Kiss Tomorrow Goodbye* (1950) and *Tony Rome* (1967), both directed by Gordon Douglas.

Tony Rome was part of a revival of the thriller that began in 1966 with Jack Smight's terrible *Harper* and terrific *Kaleidoscope;* and included Buzz Kulik's *Warning Shot* (1967) in which the best use ever was made of David Janssen's sullen mask; John Boorman's *Point Blank* (1967) in which Lee Marvin was deployed marvelously; and John Guillerin's *P.J.* in which George Peppard was used badly for the umpteenth time. Actually in the fifties and sixties television has made as good use of the detective thriller as Hollywood with such series as *The Outsider*, *Cannon*, and *Mannix*. In fact, it was the accumulated paranoia of David Janssen's television persona that made *Warning Shot* so effective. If *Colombo* owes

MARLOWE (1969). With James Garner, Kenneth Tobey, and Carroll O'Connor

a lot to Charlie Chan in his shuffling detective work, he owes even more to Chandler and Hammett for the urban landscape he inhabits and the creepy upperclass criminals he chases. Personalities as different as Craig Stevens, James Garner, and Darren McGavin owe to television whatever mythic qualities they have been able to assemble.

At least three other detective thrillers deserve special mention. *Kiss Me Deadly* (1955) was only the fifth of Robert Aldrich's films, but it is one of the best-realized in his career in genre movies, certainly the best of the Mickey Spillane pictures. What sets it apart, besides the marvel-

ous impact of its action, is the thorough way that Aldrich integrates moral questions, finally transcending genre, like all the best films about violence, to raise some deeply probing questions about the human condition.

Often overlooked in the flood of violent and sexually explicit thrillers of the late sixties are two of the most accomplished: Blake Edwards' *Gunn* (1967), starring Craig Stevens, and Paul Bogart's *Marlowe*, starring James Garner and based on *The Little Sister*, one of Chandler's finest stories. Unlike *Harper*, Jack Smight's amateurish 1966 recreation of the forties detective yarn (the

SHAMUS (1973).
With two-gun
Burt Reynolds

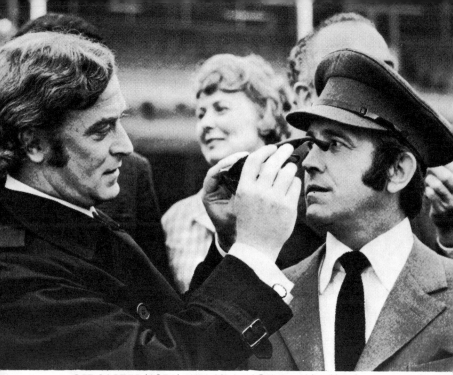
GET CARTER (1971). With Michael Caine and Ian Hendry

movie that started the revival), *Gunn* is sure, subtle, almost delicate in its use of thriller conventions of atmosphere, violence, and sex. Only in *Gunn*, for example, is the sexual aberration, in this case transvestism, an integral part of the villain's character, not just a prop. *Gunn* was a long-running television series, of course, but the movie is far more successful, although it does miss the smoldering underplaying of television's Lola Albright. Edwards captures the creeping quality of evil; like smoke, it fills every frame of the film.

Like Philip Marlowe, who was to follow him two years later, Peter Gunn is not lost in time, a forties character in a sixties world. Both detectives are played with very take-it-as-it-comes nonchalance. *Marlowe*, although not as fine a picture as Edwards', has in James Garner an authentic figure of the sixties, hip and innocent, relaxed but tough, involved but not too. (He receives superb support from Gayle Hunnicut, Sharon Farrell, Rita Moreno, and Carroll O'Connor.) His Marlowe is caught in a rush of events nearly as confusing as Bogart's—he is lied to by everyone, including his client; he is set upon by mysterious hoods, including an Oriental who chops up the furniture in his office with his hands. Nearly everyone he meets turns up with an ice pick in the back; there is not just one but three women who will either stand by him or do him in—but modern Marlowe is able to drift through it all with typical sixties insouciance. *Marlowe* was, at least for the moment, the last detective thriller. Since then every film has either been heavy-handed or funny, parody either way. (It is interesting to note that unlike Westerns, which were able to use familiar icons like Wayne, Holden, Mitchum, and Douglas as aging cowboys, there was no way to do the same with the gumshoes—Philip Marlowe started out as a tired, cynical middle-aged man.)

By the seventies we have reached some sort of watershed, and the detective thriller has degenerated into more or less conscious self-parody. An attempt at an American parody adventure was made by Buzz Kulik's *Shamus* (1973), a Burt Reynolds vehicle, but except for Reynolds himself, it wasn't long on humor.

Much funnier and much more skillful were Stephen Frears' *Gumshoe* (1971) and Michael Hodges' *Pulp* (1972). In the former Albert Finney plays a young man of the sixties, hung up on Chandler and Bogart, who deliberately involves himself in an adventure that turns out to be a lot more heartbreakingly real than he anticipates. The villainous fat man, the mysterious tail, the dangerous woman, the delicious atmosphere of shadow and menace, are all marvelously evoked. *Pulp* is a bit more serious about its fun. Michael Caine is at his usual professional best as a pulp fiction writer hired to do the memoirs of an aging movie star with Mafia connections. Figuring prominently in the cast are Mickey Rooney as the retired star, Lionel Stander as his semi-retired bodyguard, and Lizabeth Scott as his ex-wife. Caine himself is a contemporary figure in film thrillers, having established his screen personality in spy movies like *The Ipcress File* (1965) and genre films like *Get Carter*, directed by Michael Hodges in 1971.

As we shall see, this tendency to parody stretches all across the genre of the gangster film, but it is at its most successful in the thriller.

The years after World War II brought changes in Hollywood and in the nation that profoundly affected genre movies. By the late forties, the gangsters were back in full force, but they were for the most part a very different breed from their older brothers of Prohibition and the Depression. The tough Horatio Alger up-and-comer was gone, replaced by almost-respectable businessmen and psychopathic killers. The changes were brought on by an enormous alteration in the social reality, marked by the end of Prohibition and the war-inspired prosperity that ended the Depression, and by new developments within the film business itself.

American gangster films were always tied to the reality of American criminal life and the new modes of gangster operations were integrated quickly into the pattern of the genre films. Gambling and labor racketeering became the dominant forms of mob activity and soon the screens were filled with tough-talking dock workers, truck drivers, and goons, and with slick nightclub owners operating back rooms with crooked wheels and marked decks. With the smashing of the national murder franchise by a Brooklyn D.A. named Burton

THE POSTWAR GANGSTER FILM

Turkus, another dimension of the magnitude of gang behavior impressed itself upon the public and affected gangster movies. In addition, the revelations of the Kefauver committee gave support to the idea that organized crime in America was a highly structured conspiracy that was indeed national in scope. There appeared to be a network of criminal associations, all equally dedicated to making money and not afraid to divide the national pie' systematically rather than waste time and resources competing for control. The authorities have always ascribed dark motives to gangsters who infiltrate honest businesses, but from the mob point of view it was the natural thing to do, since it lowered overhead for lawyers, graft to policemen and politicians, and so on; the only fast rule was to maintain profits.

With the establishment of the image of "the syndicate," the movies began to incorporate new conventions from the folkloric traditions of these transplanted European societies. The organization was seen as held together as much by oaths of loyalty and brotherhood as by fear and profit. Silence in the face of public authority was one symbol of criminal unity. Another, far more primitive, was the kiss supposedly given to a victim by his executioner. This vocabulary of secret ceremony and primitive ritual added to the menace implicit in organization even if the mob was in reality nothing more than a slightly more venal cartel. A cartel run by armed savages instead of Harvard graduates is truly frightening.

The war had forced centralization of the government on a scale never before seen in this country and in some quarters, especially the business community which was taking the opportunity to do a little centralizing itself, "organization" was tending to take on value as a goal, regardless of to what use the organization was put. The process continued to accelerate, and state and municipal governments did their best to imitate the federal government. Concomitantly, bigness began to have similar positive connotations. Organization on an enormous scale had defeated the Nazis and now it began to change the face of America. A very visible and desirable result, for example, was the network of federally sponsored highways that began to knit the country together. It was easy to imagine that gangsters might see in bigness and organization answers to their problems, too.

Also, the postwar years were hothouses of conspiracy. The Russians and their allies conspired to take over Europe and their domestic underground conspired to help them. The Democrats conspired in "twenty years of treason" to get us into Korea. It wasn't long before Senator Joseph McCarthy and his henchmen were waving lists around proving conspiracies peppered the government, the Army, Hollywood, the universities, and probably the local grocery store. Hollywood, in particular, was alerted to the conspiracies since it was accused of harboring within its bosom one of the most dangerous and pervasive of all. It was natural for the mob, under these circumstances, to be seen as an enormous, powerful, and secret conspiracy of crime.

The intellectual atmosphere of America—and of Hollywood—had altered in other ways. Hollywood had been changed, for instance, by the arrival of a number of directors—Robert Siodmak, Fritz Lang, and Billy Wilder, for example, who had fled Europe before the spreading

WHITE HEAT (1949). With Virginia Mayo and James Cagney

stain of Nazism. They had come of age in the insecurity of Europe between the wars and they were not affected by the congenital optimism of American directors like Frank Capra or John Ford. The straightforwardness of an isolated America began to give way to the ambiguities of a United States actively engaged in running the world.

The mind of America was changing in other ways, too. The forties was the decade in which psychiatry had its major impact on this country and that impact was nowhere greater than in films. The ambiguities of the political and social situation were reflected in the ambiguous attitude that began to be taken towards the motivations of others with whom contact was made. What could be seen as charismatic energy in the Cagney of *The Public Enemy* became the psychosis in the Cagney of Raoul Walsh's *White Heat* (1949). As extreme mental states became common in genre films, the major effect was to underline the already established feeling of generalized instability that characterized the thrillers. What had been odd tics in a character's personality now became clues to his relationship with his mother. The long-range effect was to make genre films even more scarifying than they already were.

All of these developments served to feed a growing mood of skepticism both in Hollywood and in society at large. As life seemed less and less real, or as it seemed less and less possible to really grasp what life was all about, the violence and alienation of the gangster film deepened, blackened. For all its insecurity and menace, the world inhabited by Philip Marlowe in *The Big Sleep* just wasn't that bad. The sense of hopelessness and decay, of alienation and danger became almost tangible in the darkest films of the late forties and early fifties.

The new mood began to establish itself almost immediately. If *The Maltese Falcon* began the forties, it also carried over, especially in its mood, many of the attributes of the thirties. In Frank Tuttle's *This Gun For Hire* (1942), the movie that made him a star, Alan Ladd played a paid tough, in the process neatly turning the association of crime with physical ab-

THIS GUN FOR HIRE (1941). With Alan Ladd and Veronica Lake

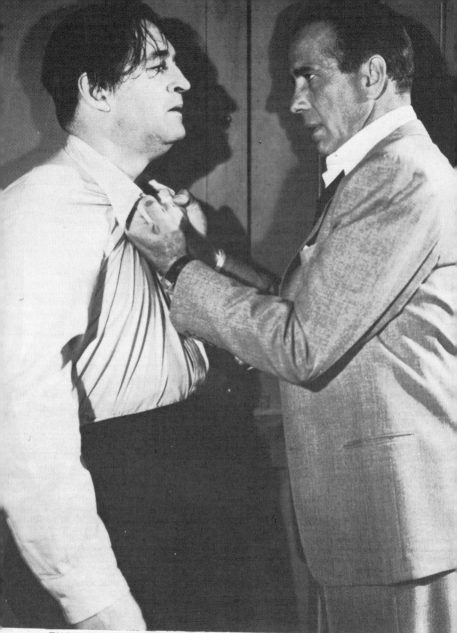

THE ENFORCER (1951). With Ted De Corsia and Humphrey Bogart

THE STREET WITH NO NAME (1948). With Donald Buka, Richard Widmark and Mark Stevens

normality on its head. Later the same year, in Stuart Heisler's version of Dashiell Hammett's *The Glass Key*, he was back on the right side of the moral Great Divide, insofar as morality plays much of a part in Hammett's cynical, ambiguous creations. A year later, John Garfield, in Richard Wallace's *The Fallen Sparrow*, played a battered Spanish Civil War veteran for whom virtue is no reward. These and other thrillers established a new mood that was carried over into the revived gangster films after the war, a mood more deeply pessimistic than any that had preceded it.

The new criminal-hero was best represented by Richard Widmark whose repressed power and paralyzing laugh smashed across his psycho in Henry Hathaway's *Kiss of Death* (1947) and his hood in William Keighley's *The Street With No Name* (1948). Gamblers were firmly established as genre types in Jacques Tourneur's tasteful melodrama *Out of the Past* (1947). Murder, Inc. made its forceful debut in *The Enforcer* (1951), with Humphrey Bogart as the

THE BIG HEAT (1953). With Lee Marvin, Gloria Grahame, and Glenn Ford

crusading D.A. and Zero Mostel in a vivid performance as a terrified "stoolie." Byron Haskin contributed one of the more effective genre pieces: *I Walk Alone* (1948), in which Burt Lancaster played an ex-con with an iron code of honor and Kirk Douglas was a socially acceptable but hopelessly corrupt businessman. Other films were spin-offs from Jules Dassin's *The Naked City* (1948): William Dieterle's *Dark City* (1950), in which Charlton Heston made his film debut; Andre de Toth's *The City Is Dark* (1954, released as *Crime Wave*), and Fritz Lang's *While the City Sleeps* (1956). A similar signal of menace was flashed by such related titles, besides Keighley's *Street With No Name*, as Anthony Mann's *Side Street* (1950), John Sturges' *Mystery Street* (1950), and Arnold Laven's *Down Three Dark Streets* (1954), not to mention Otto Preminger's *Where The Sidewalk Ends* (1950), John Huston's *Asphalt Jungle* (1950) and Laven's *Slaughter On Tenth Avenue* (1957).

The titles reinforce how important the urban scene remains in the genre. In fact the only real changes in the late forties and early fifties are quite minor: businessmen-crooks are more prominent; crooked cops and politicians are more vilely portrayed (since the introduction of the Code they had been treated quite mildly); gamblers and the technology of their trade are everywhere about; and wiretaps and electronic equipment begin to intrude. For the rest, it is a deepening of existing conventions rather than the addition of new ones that marks the changes in the genre during this period.

Central to almost every picture in the entire tradition is the action-oriented male. From the criminal to the G-man to the private investigator and onto the psychopaths of the forties and fifties, it is the man in the middle who is the focus of all the activity. His consciousness usually dominates the outlook of the movie, because action directors usually don't have the opportunity—and most seem to lack the inclination—to comment upon their characters. Most heroes in the genre are just offered up as is, without justification or explanation. There are variations of style—a Humphrey Bogart comes through almost anything unruffled, a John Garfield with cuts and bruises, but the main thrust—even in death—is a triumph of the individual male over adversity. Robert Warshow argued that we, the audience, demand the death of the gangster-hero as a reassurance of our own powerlessness. But it seems much more likely that we applaud Tom Powers or Roy Earle for putting up such a good fight, not for losing. They do what we can't: fight to the death for their identity.

From the forties on, the motivations of the characters, especially the heroes, become considerably more complex. The flawed hero, beginning with Sam Spade, is a man with rough edges. In Fritz Lang's *The Big Heat* (1953), the cop Bannion (Glenn Ford) is arrogant and vengeful, contemptuous toward authority, and ignores due process in the interest of what he sees as justice. He nearly commits murder himself as he pursues his wife's killers, but even before her death he is freely bending the rules. He is, in effect, a severely flawed character emotionally, typical of many of the movie cops of the last twenty-five years, including recent additions like Richard Widmark's *Madigan* (Don Siegel, 1968) and Gene Hackman's de-

FORCE OF EVIL (1948):
With Marie Windsor and John Garfield

MURDER, MY SWEET (1945). With Mike Mazurki, Otto Kruger, and Dick Powell

tective in William Friedkin's *The French Connection* (1972).

The criminals, on the other hand, have become more civilized. In Abraham Polonsky's *Force of Evil* (1948), John Garfield, an upwardly mobile Wall Street attorney, is hired by a gang leader to engineer the takeover of the numbers racket. The days of muscle operations are over, the film argues, and the gangsters are beginning to look and act like all the other businessmen. Polonsky's was one of the most interesting films of the period and his blacklisting was a particular sorrow in the generalized tragedy of that event. Polonsky, like Henry Hathaway in *Kiss of Death* (1947), is pitting his hero against the temptations of the world of crime. Garfield must make moral choices, a situation completely contrary to the fated careers of the classic gangsters from Tom Powers to Roy Earle. The hero presented with a moral choice becomes a central figure from this period forward and is at the core of Francis Ford Coppola's *The Godfather* (1972),

DOUBLE INDEMNITY (1944). With Barbara Stanwyck, Fred MacMurray, and Tom Powers

among others.

Something should be said about the attitude of gangster pictures toward women. These films have always been noticeably misogynist in outlook. In the thirties there were simply whores and madonnas. Mother and the little girl next door were inviolate, the rest were leeches to be used and tossed aside. In the forties a central woman character developed who had the capability of helping or hurting the hero.

In both *The Maltese Falcon* and *Murder, My Sweet* the hero's love interest turns out to be the murderer. In the fifties, ambivalence turns to hatred. Bannion in *The Big Heat* gets one woman killed and only softens towards Debbie (Gloria Grahame) after she has been badly scarred by a hood (Lee Marvin) for talking to him. Mickey Spillane's private eye, especially in *Kiss Me Deadly*, is a lot nastier than his forties counterpart, pitilessly using any woman who crosses his path.

On the other hand, by the late forties, countless films in the genre had established women as repositories of evil as well as helpless victims or ambivalent figures. Ava Gardner in Robert Siodmak's *The Killers* (1946), Lana Turner in Tay Garnett's *The Postman Always Rings Twice* (1946), and Barbara Stanwyck in Billy Wilder's *Double Indemnity* (1944, written by Wilder and Raymond Chandler from James M. Cain's novel) are all portrayed as women who ruthlessly enslave men in order to manipulate them for evil ends. In Jacques Tourneur's *Out of the Past* (1947), Jane Greer manipulates two men (Robert Mitchum and Kirk Douglas), humiliating them for years before finally running out of luck.

Changes in the business of making movies were also having an effect throughout the late forties and early fifties. It can be argued that a technical innovation, sound, made possible the gangster movie, and its emphasis on realism. Now a new invention, the wide screen, threatened to do in the genre. Actually, technology alone was not responsible for the threat. It was felt at first that the wide screen would not be suitable for the fast action

and quick cutting upon which the genre fed for its excitement, but it was quickly discovered that technically anything that was feasible before could still be done. What was different was the cost, and this, combined with a declining audience, was what gave Hollywood the jitters. One result of the business' money problems was a rapid increase in the number of independent productions. And independence meant that directors were no longer so tied to projects for which they were not suited just to fill contract obligations to studios. It meant that a number of directors who were attracted to the action film could devote themselves to the genre without interruption.

Under the old system of assigned projects it took a lucky break or an unusual amount of power for a director to get to do the films he wanted. Mervyn LeRoy had to badger the front office to get a crack at *Little Caesar*, and even then his work doesn't compare with Wellman's on *The Public Enemy* or Hawks' on *Scarface*. And almost all the major genre films through the war were by directors—Hawks (*Scarface, The Big Sleep*), Lang (*M, Fury, You Only Live Once, Man Hunt*), Huston (*The Maltese Falcon*), Walsh (*The Roar-*

THE HOUSE ON NINETY-SECOND STREET (1945). With Signe Hasso

ing Twenties, High Sierra)—who tended to have personal styles that transcended the particular material they were working from; good directors made good gangster movies. In the postwar period and into the fifties, as we shall see, a number of directors established themselves as specialists in the genre film. Not that the major directors didn't continue to make occasional forays —Lang brought off *The Big Heat* in 1953 and *Beyond a Reasonable Doubt* in 1956; Walsh

White Heat in 1949; Huston *The Asphalt Jungle* in 1950. And lesser directors who had worked the genre also continued to make movies, filmmakers like LeRoy, Gordon Douglas, William Dieterle, William Keighley, Michael Curtiz, Edward L. Cahn, and Edward Dmytryk, but at this level the only director to successfully make the switch in mood and iconography was Henry Hathaway.

Hathaway, who, like William Wellman is often underrat-

Marlowe's exploration of this city leads him, as Colin McArthur has written, "into a fragmented and incomprehensible world peopled by characters whose motivations, commitment, and sometimes precise identity, are unclear."° Marlowe must discover who has done what, and why, often without knowing for sure who or where they are. Where is Sean Regan, for example, and why is he there? What does Vivian have going with the gangster Eddie Mars and where do her sister Carmen's gambling debts fit in? What is Mars' connection to the blackmailer Geiger? And who is Harry Jones, the man who keeps tailing Marlowe? As they are in *The Maltese Falcon*, even objects are deceitful: Harry Jones is killed with cyanide masked as whiskey; the pictures of Carmen are taken by a camera hidden in a buddha; Geiger's diary is in

°Colin McArthur, *Underworld U.S.A.*, New York, The Viking Press, p. 72.

DARK CITY (1950). With Lizabeth Scott and Charlton Heston

ed because of his simplicity and straightforwardness as a director, was a fairly successful middle-rank studio craftsman who clicked in the late forties with a series of tough crime films and melodramas. Leading off was *The House On Ninety-Second Street* (1945), the first of a new sub-genre, the police documentary. This mode nearly always includes a portentous narrator emphasizing that what follows is fact; location shooting; the use of actual participants in the events wherever possible; and detailed explanations of police procedures. The movie concerned the FBI's detection of a German spy

ring in Yorktown. Hathaway followed up the next year with *13 Rue Madeleine* and *The Dark Corner* (Andrew Sarris unfairly calls the latter film a poor man's *Laura*), with *Kiss of Death* in 1947 and *Call Northside 777* in 1948. Of all his contemporaries in the studio shop, only Hathaway broke away to the extent that he could make a few startlingly well-wrought thrillers and found a mini-genre that was practically his own.

Raoul Walsh returned to the genre in 1949 with *White Heat*, one of the few films in which James Cagney received strong direction. In theme and style

KEY LARGO (1948). With Humphrey Bogart and Edward G. Robinson

White Heat is a throwback to an earlier time, a remake of the attempts to revitalize the gangster film in the late thirties. Like John Huston's *Key Largo* a year earlier, *White Heat* is the chronicle of a gangster's swan song. Both films are notable for their acting and screenplays, but neither one was representative of where the genre was at or where it was going. *White Heat* fits in somewhat with the caper movie, about to get its biggest inspiration from *The Asphalt Jungle*, but really both Huston and Walsh are reactionaries so far as their relationship to the genre.

Both of these films are notable, however, for the force of the performances of the leading and supporting actors, Cagney in *White Heat*, and Bogart and Robinson (with help from Claire Trevor and Thomas Gomez) in *Key Largo*. Cagney and Robinson, especially, underline the importance of icon-inspired responses to stars. Cagney is aided enormously by Walsh's tough direction as he wrings from the actor one of the triumphs of his career, but Robinson, too, overcoming Huston's somewhat stagy piloting, turns in one of his most memorable performances. It is as if both actors were as convinced as the audience of their gangster identities.

Fritz Lang and John Huston are not particularly associated with gangster films, but Huston has made two influential pictures in the genre and Lang's pessimistic movies have had a profound if mostly indirect influence. Lang, more than all but a few directors, had a consistent philosophical outlook that affects all of his films from *Dr. Mabuse* (1922) to *The Thousand Eyes of Dr. Mabuse* in 1961. In *Metropolis* (1926), he created a nightmare city, an absurd, fanciful, chilling world of menacing shadows. In America, where he worked after escaping Germany in 1933, he must have thought his nightmare had been realized. Running through Lang's films is a deep strain of paranoia. His obsession with the mechanics of plot marks him as a man of his century; he does not build careful sequences of action to illuminate characters, he builds traps, horrible boxes from which his characters cannot escape. He is like a designer of very abstruse and pessimistic games.

In Lang's *Beyond A Reasonable Doubt* (1956), a newspaper publisher (Sidney Blackmer) who opposes capital punishment sets out to prove that an innocent man could easily be convicted and put to death. When a showgirl is found strangled, the

THE ASPHALT JUNGLE (1950). With Sterling Hayden, Brad Dexter, Louis Calhern, and Sam Jaffe

publisher persuades his future son-in-law, Tom Garrett (Dana Andrews), to play guilty and leaves innumerable clues at the site of the crime, in his car. He also has Garrett deny that he has an alibi. The publisher documents the frame-up. Garrett is arrested, tried, convicted, and sentenced to death. On his way to the D.A.'s office with the evidence, the publisher is killed in an accident and the proof of innocence destroyed. Garrett's fiancée (Joan Fontaine) believes him innocent and investigates the dead girl's past. Meanwhile, the publisher's safe is opened, copies of the evidence of the frame are discovered, and Garrett is reprieved. But he has mentioned the showgirl's original name to his fiancée and she, realizing that he has in fact been guilty all along, denounces him and he is executed.

The plot sounds extremely artificial, but it is consistent with Lang's preoccupation with the processes of detection and conviction, that is, with responsibility. His characters struggle mightily against the fates and yet in the end are usually tripped up accidentally and inevitably by their moral flaws. Lang's perspective and the unique success he had at expressing it deeply affected films, especially thrillers.

John Huston's best film was *The Asphalt Jungle* (1950). Like *The Maltese Falcon*, this first important caper movie benefits from a superb cast that included Sterling Hayden, James Whitmore, Jean Hagen, Sam Jaffe, Louis Calhern, and Marilyn Monroe in one of her best early roles. (Sam Jaffe was especially fine as an aging but lecherous gang member.) The film's most significant attribute was that it tended to make the characters more three-dimensional than traditional gangster films, but this is in part due to the nature of the caper as a convention. The persons who are assembled for capers are usually there for reasons very different from the power trip of a Little Caesar. In *The Asphalt Jungle*, one seeks retirement in a Mexican nirvana, another escape from the United States. A third has too many mouths to feed. And the leader, Dix (Hayden) wants to go where everybody knows you can't, namely, home again. (Mortally wounded, he dies in the peaceful fields of his old farm, surrounded by his beloved horses.) Capers are played out against an absence of right and wrong. In most cases, there is an inevitability to their hopelessness, although in the sixties there are a few capers that succeed.

These are the old-style directors whose work continued to be important into the postwar years, where they strengthened and reinforced the conventions of the classic gangster film. But as films moved into the fifties and sixties, the gangster film splintered off into many subgenres: gangster melodramas, new and old style; rural bandit stories like *Dillinger*; police documentaries; thrillers of every description. The scene began to be dominated by a number of younger directors whose work in the gangster genre was much more violent, much more sexually explicit, and much more extreme in outlook. A number of these directors should be looked at individually to determine what went on in the fifties and sixties.

In the thirties, a director, like his producer, his screenwriter, and his stars, was a creature of the studio that employed him. If his luck or his talent was extraordinary, he might get to work on projects that he cared about, but most directors did what they were told to do, a gangster movie this week, a musical next, a Western after that. By the sixties, the situation had changed completely; productions were set up and financed independently, often by directors themselves, like Robert Aldrich after the success of *What Ever Happened to Baby Jane?* and *Hush, Hush . . . Sweet Charlotte*, and distributed by the old studios. Nowhere is this more true than in the genre films—the gangster films, the Westerns, the war films, etc—which, when they come out anymore, are far more likely to be the products of independent producers and directors.

Increasingly after the war, movies were dominated by a group of filmmakers who, for one reason or another, made their mark working steadily in all or several of the various genres. Some preferred to be there, some became mired in relatively low-budget films because the disdain of the American critics and much of the film audience prevented

THE VIOLENT YEARS— THE GANGSTER FILM IN THE FIFTIES AND SIXTIES

their virtues as directors from being widely appreciated.

Almost all of them had several attitudes in common: they usually saw America as an extremely corrupt and/or violent place and they tended to have a striking visual style at the same time that they were not very interested in the refinements of storytelling or the subtleties of argument. Inevitably, the gangster film had a special attraction for them: the gangster dispensing brutality and mayhem was an appropriate symbol for a country which sanctioned crime in the national interest and looked away from the poverty and the alienation that bred murderous activity.

What follows is a summary of twelve directors who have deeply affected the development of the gangster film in the last quarter century. Some of the names are well-known, some not, but all are names that, when they appear above the title, should attract our attention. They are discussed in alphabetical order because there seems to be no more satisfactory way of

THE GARMENT JUNGLE (1957). With Richard Boone and Lee J. Cobb

listing them. Any ten people would probably rate them differently qualitatively, and chronologically they overlap where they are not parallel.

One of the most widely discussed genre directors is Robert Aldrich who has made several grimly effective melodramas: *The Big Knife*, 1955; *What Ever Happened to Baby Jane?* 1962; *The Dirty Dozen*, 1967. Although he was made only two movies immediately important to this study, *Kiss Me Deadly* (1955), and *The Garment Jungle* (1957), his harsh, garish style has been widely imitated. *The Gar-* *ment Jungle* is especially interesting, a swift-moving, bone-hard tale of skulduggery in the garment industry that has been officially credited to Vincent Sherman but which, according to all reliable reports, is almost all Aldrich's. The movie's basic framework is familiar—the conflict of a father and son (Lee J. Cobb and Kerwin Mathews) over encroaching gang terrorism in their business—but key elements show evidence of the fifties' emphasis on explicit violence and mental aberration: a terrifying murder in an elevator and Richard Boone's patently unstable

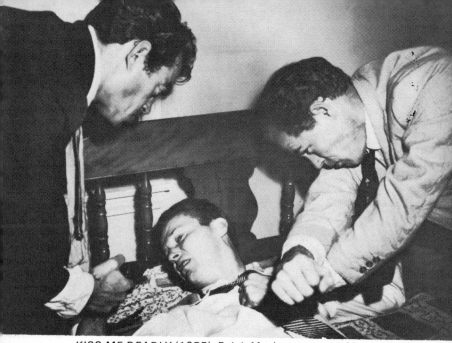

KISS ME DEADLY (1955). Ralph Meeker gets a working-over

behavior as the kingpin gangster are only two of these elements. Ralph Meeker's pathologically self-centered character in *Kiss Me Deadly* is another example of Aldrich's fascination with extremes of character, which is matched by a visual style that is equally extreme, all jangly and unpredictable. Aldrich sees the world as a modern, post-Nuremberg, post-Hiroshima version of Warshow's city, mirrored perfectly in a jumpy style.

Budd Boetticher is probably as little known as Robert Aldrich is famous. He began his career in 1951 with a respectably received but not very exciting film, *The Bullfighter and the Lady*, then found himself as an artist with a striking style of Western in the middle of the decade. *The Man from the Alamo* (1953) was a particularly strong movie about a tight-lipped survivor of the Alamo massacre (Glenn Ford), who is accused of cowardly desertion. Since that time, Boetticher has come up with a classic in the gangster mode, *The Rise and Fall of Legs Diamond* (1960), a throwback to the gangster films of Prohibition-Depression days that follows convention so rigidly it settles its protagonist's fate

THE RISE AND FALL OF LEGS DIAMOND (1960). With Ray Danton and Jesse White (seated)

THE RISE AND FALL OF LEGS DIAMOND (1960). Ray Danton as Legs Diamond shoots it out.

THE ST. VALENTINE'S DAY MASSACRE (1967).
Massacre in a Chicago garage, 1929

right in the title. Ray Danton played Diamond, a tricky opportunist and cold-blooded killer whose rise from small-time thief to personal bodyguard to gambler Arnold Rothstein (Robert Lowery) is traced against well-rendered backgrounds of the twenties. The film benefited from Joseph Landon's tight screenplay and from Boetticher's able direction, which captured some of the tense, swift action of the old Cagney-Robinson films. Boetticher's style is clean and forceful; *Legs Diamond*, which demands some pretty messy behavior from its characters, is direct and unflinching in reporting upon them. He is a singular-

ly realistic director in a mode noted for realism.

Almost all the important directors of genre pictures are noticeably more proficient with the visual aspects of moviemaking than with such matters as continuity or acting. In some cases these talents become absurdly one-sided, as with producer-director Roger Corman whose series of horror and monster movies for American International Pictures were as visually arresting as they were devoid of ideas or meaning. (An exception was *X, The Man with the X-Ray Eyes*, released in 1963.) Corman brought his self-conscious, almost painterly style to Twentieth-Century Fox when they asked him to direct *The St. Valentine's Day Massacre* (1967), which climaxed with the bloody and notorious murder of an entire Chicago gang in 1929. With a fairly large budget, Corman was able to beautifully recreate the look of the twenties in postcard colors, but the film had a monotonous and pointless screenplay by Howard Browne and was foolishly overplayed by Jason Robards (as Al Capone), George Segal, Ralph Meeker, and Jean Hale. Surprisingly, out of a series of blood-splattered shootouts, the one effective sequence involved the brutal beating of Jean Hale by George Segal. The massacre itself was elaborately staged, but in a typical lapse of tastè, Corman allowed the camera to linger on the curls of smoke from the shotgun that had just completed the massacre.

Although he isn't much of a thinker, Corman is fairly ambitious to be one and frequently takes on current events and issues, often in a way that is more powerful in its naïveté and the

BLOODY MAMA (1970). With Clint Kimbrough, Shelley Winters, and Robert Walden

THE NAKED CITY (1948). Ted De Corsia flees from the New York police.

immediacy of its visuals than pictures by more thoughtful filmmakers [cf., race relations: *The Intruder* (1955); bikers: *The Wild Angels* (1966); the drug experience: *The Trip* (1967).] It is evidence of Corman's concerns and proof of his abilities that he can consistently use actors as wooden as Peter Fonda as he then was and William Shatner as he always is and still come up with films that are worth seeing. His crime movies, including *Bloody Mama* (1970), with Shelley Winters as Ma Barker, have the same untroubled and unambiguous directness. Also, like Aldrich, Corman has a repertory company of character actors (notably Leo Gordon and Bruce Dern) who appear in many of his

films and give them added resonance.

Jules Dassin is not so much a good director as one who has made some interesting and influential movies. If one did not know in advance, however, it would be hard to match his creations to him, since they lack a convincing personal visual style. Three of his movies are important to the history of the gangster movie, the least famous being the best. In its use of actual New York City settings to relate a conventional tale of the police's pursuit and capture of a killer, Dassin's *The Naked City* (1948) was seminal in the development of the iconography of the modern gangster film. By permitting the cameras to

NIGHT AND THE CITY (1950). With Richard Widmark and Gene Tierney

wander through the police stations, tenements, playgrounds, docks, and bridges of the city, the film achieved a certain forcefulness weakened by the routine story and by Barry Fitzgerald's overplayed and miscast police captain. In retrospect, one wonders how much of the forcefulness was Dassin's doing and how much the responsibility of producer Mark Hellinger who put together many of the films that dominated the genre.

Dassin's *Rififi* (1956), one of the first big caper movies, had the interesting effect of making its audiences feel like accomplices to the crime before visiting retribution on the criminals, but, except for the long silent robbery sequence, it seems less an important film than it must have fifteen years ago. Only *Night and the City* (1950), a Langian excursion into a surrealistic city of nightmare and terror, retains its impact. Of all the screen images of the early fifties, Richard Widmark's terrorized Fabian in *Night and the City*, fleeing from grotesques both physical (Frank L. Sullivan) and psychological (Herbert Lom), is among the most memorable. In Europe, Dassin is considered a major directorial talent, though it is impossible to say why. He may be one of the few people for whom the blacklist was a lucky break.

Within the discipline of the genre there lurks an occasional genius. One such genius was Fritz Lang, who never allowed genre conventions to limit his style or content. Another lesser and very different but still superb film creator is Samuel Fuller whose list of thrillers, gangster and war movies, and Westerns includes a phenomenal number of unforgettable works, phenomenal, especially, for a director who is virtually unknown. Fuller is a raw primitive, not technically —he is an accomplished film-maker—but artistically, intellectually. He has a few simple concerns upon which he concentrates an enormous artistry; his view of life is elemental and he expresses it with perfect, not to say awesome power.

The list of Fuller's films is impressive even when, for the purpose of this account, it is limited to his crime pictures. *Pickup on South Street* (1953), which Fuller wrote as well as directed, was a brutal melodrama about a nasty thug (Richard Widmark) who becomes involved with Communist spies. In a series of violent sequences, the murder of stool pigeon Thelma Ritter was staged outstandingly well by the director. *House of Bamboo* (1955) was a colorful film concerning the exposure and capture of a group of ex-G.I. criminals working in and around

PICKUP ON SOUTH STREET (1953). With Jean Peters and Richard Widmark

HOUSE OF BAMBOO (1955). With De Forest Kelley, Robert Stack and Robert Ryan

Tokyo after World War II. Fuller took a leaf from Aldrich's book in the clear suggestion that the criminal leader (Robert Ryan) was mentally unstable and one from Dassin's book in his use of actual Tokyo locales for his big sequences. *The Crimson Kimono* (1959) and *Shock Corridor* (1963) also had effective moments, but best of all was *Underworld U.S.A.* (1961), an uncommonly powerful gangster movie concerning a man's relentless search for his father's murderers. Cliff Robertson was fine as the man who promises forgiveness to a dying witness in return for the killers' names, then mutters "Sucker!" as the witness dies.

It is a commonplace that artists, especially visual artists, are not always intellectuals. Fuller has few of what can arguably be identified as ideas, but unlike Corman neither has he pretensions; he is almost a pure artist. A Boetticher or a Phil Karlson may be weakened by a lack of critical response, but Fuller works so close to the main vein of his talent that he has suffered no loss by not being hailed as the great film artist that he is. The only real tragedy lies with those who have missed the joy of experiencing his films.

Phil Karlson is not a film creator of the magnitude of Sam Fuller, but he deserves an impor-

UNDERWORLD, U.S.A. (1961). With Dolores Dorn and Cliff Robertson

TIGHT SPOT (1955). With Edward G. Robinson and Ginger Rogers

tant place in this narrative. The most significant aspect of Karlson's crime films has been a deep streak of ambiguity in his attitude toward the situations of both the criminals and their victims. Ambiguity is an important attitude of the postwar gangster movie, and no one is more divided about the moral and social implications of action-dominated characters than Karlson. In *Kansas City Confidential* (1952), for example, not only is most of the violence committed by the hero (John Payne), bent on clearing himself of a robbery charge, but there are clear implications that the Kansas City police are a nasty and sadistic lot. And in *Tight Spot* (1955), the policeman (Brian Keith) assigned to guard a beautiful material witness (Ginger Rogers) is actually in the pay of the gang lords and has been ordered to kill her. There has also been a streak of social criticism in Karlson that has led him to such themes as the mistreatment of Japanese-Americans during World War II (*Hell to Eternity*, 1960) and the role of the concerned citizen in the fight against crime (*The Phenix City Story*, 1955). His best film is a gangster melodrama, *The Brothers Rico* (1957), an uncompromising movie that, like *The Rise and Fall of Legs Dia-*

BOOMERANG (1947). With Guy Thomajan, Lee J. Cobb, and Dana Andrews

mond, beautifully reworks many of the genre's hoariest conventions, including in this instance a revered mother as in *White Heat* and an avenging enemy like Bannion in *The Big Heat*.

Elia Kazan is a not very entertaining but important director whose career has included at least three memorable crime action efforts: *Boomerang* (1947), *Panic in the Streets* (1950), and *On the Waterfront* (1954). All three use conventions of the gangster film to work out some of Kazan's "broader" concerns. In *Boomerang* and *On the Waterfront*, the central character must choose between truth and his own safety and well-being. (In the first it is a district attorney suffering withering pressure to convict an innocent man, in the second a punch-drunk, third-rate fighter who must give evidence against the labor boss who runs his neighborhood.) In *Panic in the Streets* a public health official must move against official resistance, as in *Boomerang*, to find the killers of a carrier of plague who lives in a dockside immigrant community, as in *On the Waterfront*. Kazan handles genre conventions well enough— the familiar trappings of gang

ON THE WATERFRONT (1954). With Marlon Brando

betrayal and assassination are especially vivid in *On the Waterfront*—but his real strength is with actors, and it is here that his films are important. The characters that he created with Marlon Brando, Lee J. Cobb, Richard Widmark, Rod Steiger, and Dana Andrews broadened considerably the vocabulary of portrayal for gangster figures. It is also possible that Kazan had a steadying effect on the excesses of some of his contemporaries. His films stand out for the static nature of the framing and cutting, like Huston's, without being the least bit dull, and he serves as a reminder of the possibilities present in careful plotting and playing. It may be that, like Fritz Lang, Kazan was reaching for deeper meanings than usually found in genre movies, but unlike the German master, he lacked the ability as a filmmaker to carry it off.

Another strenuously overlooked director comes from a slightly older generation: Joseph

GUN CRAZY (1950). With Peggy Cummins and John Dall

RAW DEAL (1948). Dennis O'Keefe as Joe Sullivan

H. Lewis' first film was in 1937 and by 1950 he had made several compelling films, including *Gun Crazy* (1950), a marvelously subtle and evocative version of the Bonnie and Clyde legend, with John Dall and Peggy Cummins. The previous year he made *The Undercover Man*, with Glenn Ford as a Treasury Department cop pursuing tax violators, and in 1955 he directed *The Big Combo*, using Cornel Wilde more successfully than might have been dreamed possible. Lewis has a complex visual style, as intricate as Fuller's is direct, and fully as beautiful and effective. His subject specialty is neurotic sexuality, often given poetically provocative presentation, as in the bizarre but lasting relationship between Cummins and Dall. But sexuality is the flaw as often as it is the salvation of his creatures: Wilde's crusading cop is done in by his obsession with a dancer. And Lewis uses sexual distress to create some of the most lasting and compelling images in film: for example, the scene in *My Name is Julia Ross* (1945) in which George Macready savagely shreds Nina Foch's underwear with a razor. As with Fuller, there is probably not a single film of Lewis' that does not contain within it at least a few minutes of classic filmmaking.

Anthony Mann was a relatively minor director of gangster films, although a somewhat more important creator of Westerns (*Winchester 73*, 1950; *Bend of the River*, 1952, etc.) but his several gangster films have a gritty realism that makes them quite interesting. His gangster films are on the whole more personal than his Westerns, most of which were shaped by his partnership with James Stewart. In the vigorous *T-Men* (1948), with Dennis O'Keefe as a determined Treasury man uncovering a nest of thieves, he drew exceptionally strong performances from Wallace Ford as an underworld schemer and John Wengraf as an urbane crook. *Raw Deal* (1948) involved fugitive-on-the-run Dennis O'Keefe with two women (Claire Trevor and Marsha Hunt). Two of Mann's best were *Border Incident* (1949), with George Murphy and Ricardo Montalban as Immigration Department officers working to stop the illegal immigration of Mexican peasants into the United States; and *Side Street* (1950), concerning a young mailman (Farley Granger) who ventures into crime with disastrous results. This film ended with a vividly photographed chase in downtown New York.

BORDER INCIDENT (1949). With George Murphy, Howard da Silva, and
Charles McGraw

Although perhaps not as great a figure as Fuller or Lewis, Nicholas Ray is a major creator of action films. Like Mann, Boetticher, and Karlson, his failure to expand outside of genre conventions has led to the critical deep-freeze, but he has chosen, instead of decline, to absent himself from Hollywood. Like Lewis, his theme is often sexuality, but he is more interested in the hope it brings outcasts than in the workings of the distorted psyches themselves. Like Lewis, he reworked the Bonnie and Clyde theme in *They Live By Night* (1949), this time with Farley Granger and Cathy O'Donnell. Not surprisingly, given the naïveté with which the director draws his couple, Lewis' is by far the more stimulating. Still, Ray's doomed Keechie and Bowie evoke concern and compassion as they flee from one bleak tourist camp or motel to another.

As with Mann, Fuller, and Lewis, no Ray film can be ignored entirely: the ambiguity he attaches to living and his handling of the screen image make him one of the most interesting directors of gangster films. *On Dangerous Ground* (1952) provides Robert Ryan with one of

THEY LIVE BY NIGHT (1949). With Farley Granger and Cathy O'Donnell

ON DANGEROUS GROUND (1952). With Robert Ryan, Ward Bond, and Ida Lupino

PARTY GIRL (1958). With Lee J. Cobb, Robert Taylor, John Ireland, and Cyd Charisse

MADIGAN (1968). With Richard Widmark and Harry Guardino

his better roles as a detective turned sadist out of bitterness and hate, who learns generosity from a murderer's blind sister (Ida Lupino). *Party Girl* (1958), part of the Prohibition-Depression cycle, offers Robert Taylor as the crippled "mouthpiece" for a mob who finds romance with a downtrodden dancer (Cyd Charisse) and finally opposes gang leader Lee J. Cobb, in a role he can play by now by just standing still. Ray is particularly good at violence, real or threatened, but especially the latter. Like Lang and Lewis, he knows that images can be conjured that will bring the impact of violence home emphatically without having actually to show it committed, as when Lee J. Cobb pours acid on a Christmas bauble the same color as Cyd Charisse's dress. Ray also has a fully realized concept of mise-en-scène. His sets, costumes, lighting, etc., are flawlessly chosen to advance the action. It is everyone's loss and no one's gain that Ray is able to find more satisfaction making underground films than he could when he had Hollywood's production and distribution facilities at his disposal.

Don Siegel is one of the few genre directors besides Aldrich to achieve a measure of security and fame. If Siegel has a particular genius, it is editing. His films are noted for their superior pace and the excitement of their finales (cf., the excellent action montage at the end of *Madigan*). The typical Siegel hero is a loner, more often than not a criminal, or a proto-criminal like the cops in *Madigan* or *Coogan's Bluff* (1968), trying to adjust to what is an unsparingly normal world. Unlike most other genre filmmakers, Siegel does not present his characters' vision or some approximation thereof on the screen; the action, as distorted as it may be, takes place in an environment, moral and physical, that is clearly recognizable as the same one we all inhabit. His best films have included *Baby Face Nelson* (1957), in which Mickey Rooney chewed his way through the title role and Sir Cedric Hardwicke won acting honors as an alcoholic doctor, and the 1964 version of *The Killers*, a cheaply made, explicitly violent transformation of the Hemingway story, inferior to the 1946 film by Robert Siodmak.

Siodmak, another German émigré who found that he could produce satisfying film melodrama within the Hollywood limitations, is a director whose historical career belongs exclusively to the forties, although he made films from 1927 to the present.

THE KILLERS (1946). With Jeff Corey, Burt Lancaster, Albert Dekker, and Ava Gardner

Although his mise-en-scène resembles Lang's, Siodmak is only interested in action. His characters are for the most part more depraved than those of the other directors covered here, as if pathological personalities were the only ones that Siodmak found interesting. Although Siodmak's important crime-action period ran only from 1945 (*The Suspect*) to 1949 (*Criss Cross*), his combination of slick production and obsessional content had a deep influence on the genre. *The Killers* (1946) moved from a perfect rendition of Hemingway's short story to a tangled but gripping tale of treachery and deceit in which Burt Lancaster made an impressive debut as the doomed Swede. *Cry of the City* (1948) was a tough melodrama that added a measure of conviction and reality to the familiar story of two young men from the same neighborhood who end up opposing each other in a violent shootout. Victor Mature played the honorable police lieutenant who must hunt down killer Richard Conte. Siodmak's *Criss Cross*

CRISS CROSS (1949). With Yvonne de Carlo, Burt Lancaster
and Dan Duryea

THE GEORGE RAFT STORY (1961). With Ray Danton and Neville Brand

MURDER, INC. (1960). With Peter Falk, May Britt, and Stuart Whitman

(1949) had Burt Lancaster as a man perilously involved with a double-crossing woman (Yvonne de Carlo) and the painstakingly planned robbery of an armored truck. The climactic scene in which the gang assaults the truck equipped with guns, tear gas bombs, and gas masks, is brilliantly carried out by the director.

This short list of directors, while it contains the major directors within the genre, cannot claim to cover more than a fraction of the directors who contributed works of lasting importance. Others who deserve mention, some of them accomplished in other modes, are: André de Toth (*Crime Wave*, 1954); John Boorman (for the marvelous and so far unique "cool" of *Point Blank*, 1967); Buzz Kulik (*Warning Shot*, 1967); Irving Lerner (*Murder By Contract*, 1958); Stuart Rosenberg (*Murder, Inc.*, 1960, with Burt Balaban); Paul Wendkos (especially *The Case Against Brooklyn*, 1958); Joseph M. Newman (*The George Raft Story*, 1961); Joseph Pevney (*Six Bridges to Cross*, 1955); Rudolph Maté (*D.O.A.*,1950); and Bernard Girard (*Dead Heat on a Merry-Go-Round*, 1966). Of course, this accounting does not include the contributions of producers, actors, screenwriters, and cameramen, but it does allow a way of tracing some of the finer gangster movies of the fifties and sixties.

Hard-as-nails, usually uncompromising, and brutal, these films took advantage of sophisticated new techniques in cinémaphotography to create a dazzling, explosive milieu in which their corrupt cops, psychotic hoods, and deceitful women could flourish. Frequently, they sacrificed the deeper, subtler meanings of the older gangster films for pyrotechnic "effects." Frequently, their brutality was pointless or gratuitous. But the tawdry, dangerous, amoral world they vivified was undeniably compelling.

The last decade has seen the arrival of two major critical and financial successes and some few other *succès d'estime*. Few people missed Arthur Penn's sensational *Bonnie and Clyde* (1967), the movie that caps, probably for all time, the lyrical-romantic approach to the lives of gangsters. And there is hardly anyone who missed *The Godfather* (1972), Francis Ford Coppola's mock panegyric to old movies and old values.

Bonnie and Clyde grows out of and amplifies a poetic tradition going back to *The Public Enemy*. It fuses the romance of *You Only Live Once* or *Gun Crazy* with the energy of a *Night and the City* or *Madigan*, serving them up with a pacing and authority, a brilliance, that its director showed neither before nor since. *The Godfather* is the end of a trail that leads back from the grim sensationalism of *The St. Valentine's Day Massacre* through the self-conscious realism of the police documentary to the bitter truth of *Scarface*. *Bonnie and Clyde* is an original screenplay; *The Godfather* was a best-selling novel. Both movies falsify the traditions from which they spring.

Both films caused sensation at the time of their release. *Bonnie and Clyde* struck at a mo-

BONNIE, CLYDE, AND DON CORLEONE

ment when the American product was being overshadowed by European cinema, at least insofar as the critical community and the media were concerned. Its arty, Europeanized use of violence made it one of the most debated films of the decade. By the time of *The Godfather*, samurai films, spaghetti Westerns, and Sam Peckinpah had made extremes of violence commonplace and the real debate came down to whether or not it was much of a movie. It was, without doubt, big news. Adapted from one of the most commercially potent popular novels of all time (by Mario Puzo, who also did the screenplay with Coppola), it turned into the biggest moneymaker in movie history.

The Godfather, in interesting contrast to *Bonnie and Clyde*, is not an especially well-written movie, nor does Coppola's directing have much drive. The only moments of the film that come alive visually are the bits of gratuitous violence. Most of it is staged and paced like a competent television melodrama. It is well-enough acted for the

BONNIE AND CLYDE (1967). With Faye Dunaway and Warren Beatty

most part, although, except for Al Pacino, most of these actors have been better in other roles. It was marketed beautifully, of course, especially with regard to Marlon Brando whose supporting role was manipulated into an Academy Award for Best Actor. But it is more like a series of pretty watercolors, with one carefully posed but two-dimensional scene after another, than it is like a film. It seems to be conceived in the misapprehension that you humanize a character if you make him boring. *Mannix* and *Colombo* do a better job with the banality-of-evil number on a fraction of the budget. Its weaknesses were no doubt the source of its strength in the marketplace; it was tailor-made for an audience that bestows its loudest applause on *Love Story* and *Jonathan Livingston Seagull*.

Bonnie and Clyde is a flawed creation too, but in its ambitions and its faults it is a very different kind of film than *The Godfather*. The source of most of the picture's failures is in the inconsistency of the visions of the director and the screenwriters. Benton and Newman had written a script that cried for hard, realistic direction;

THE GODFATHER (1972) Marlon Brando as Don Corleone

BONNIE AND CLYDE (1967). With Faye Dunaway and Warren Beatty

instead they got from Penn a bloody *Umbrellas of Cherbourg*. But Penn's visuals are brilliant, and the screen is alive with excitement from beginning to end. If Warren Beatty and Faye Dunaway are amateurish, if details as important as the characters' sex life are left unresolved, it almost doesn't matter. Penn thrilled and excited his audience and that's what motion pictures are all about.

It is far more understandable that *Bonnie and Clyde* was objected to for its handling of violence than that *The Godfather*

was able to pretty much escape criticism. Violence is one of the fundamental elements of the gangster movie, but traditionally it was used in a way that even if it wasn't set at a distance from the audience, as in Nicholas Ray's films where the violent acts often seem to come out of or towards the audience, it at least was experienced in a comfortable format. *Bonnie and Clyde* removed the conventions that provided that safety; as Pauline Kael noted, each bit of violence comes in the middle of a laugh, a sickening slap in the face when you

THE GODFATHER (1972). With Al Pacino, Marlon Brando, James Caan, and Al Lettieri

least expect it. Bonnie and Clyde as played by Warren Beatty and Faye Dunaway, are innocent and playful, but their fun results in others having their faces blown apart.

The violence in *The Godfather* is of an opposite sort, neither implicative nor purgative, but entirely exploitive in intent and effect. Each movie has a dance of death in which gunfire keeps bodies moving in the air long after they are dead. In *Bonnie and Clyde*, it is the protagonists dancing their last gay dance together in front of the policemen who have come to bring society's retribution. James Caan's Sonny is merely a victim in a gang war and his death would have been as effective in advancing the plot and motivating his survivors if it had occurred off-screen. When Tom Powers murdered Putty Nose in *The Public Enemy* the impact of that act was not lost because it was not

ferred to because she has been there a long time. Coppola uses icons like cars and guns as if he is doing a promotion film for an antique gallery; each carefully framed set looks like a showroom window. The only time this breaks down is in his flashy use of violence, but although this seems compelling by comparison to the rest of the movie, it too is stagy without attendant visual benefits. (Compare, for example, the bullet through the eyeglasses here with the beautiful/horrible image of the sprawled motor-cyclist with smashed goggles in Don Siegel's version of *The Killers.*)

In the ways they use gang-ster film conventions, the two films are nearly opposites. Penn was working in a sub-genre, the boundaries of which are, admit-tedly, less clearly defined than in the classic mode pursued by Coppola. But even allowing for that difference, Penn pulls all stops, arguably in the wrong di-rection (away from the brutal conviction of the script), but nonetheless stretching the limits of our perceptions, testing him-self and the material. *The Godfa-ther*, on the other hand, always plays it safe. It would never occur to Coppola, evidently, to stage a scene such as the one in *The Brotherhood* (1968) when

seen by the audience.

Even aside from such mat-ters as pacing, the handling of iconographic material is far surer and more evocative in Penn's movie than Coppola's. When Bonnie visits her mother, at a family picnic, it is a central event of the film, reinforcing Bonnie's humanity and mortality the way Cagney's relationship to his mother does in *White Heat*. The mother in *The Godfather* is a cardboard figure who gets de-

THE BROTHERHOOD (1968). With Luther Adler and Kirk Douglas

director Martin Ritt has Kirk Douglas, playing an aging *capo*, plant his own death kiss, boldly altering a gangster film cliché to illustrate a character. In *The Godfather*, the clichés are just clichés.

The Brotherhood and another movie from the same period point up some of the ways in which *The Godfather* and *Bonnie and Clyde* go wrong. In *Bloody Mama* (1970), Roger Corman depicts the same world of small-time, mid-West banditry for which Penn strove, and Martin Ritt's *The Brotherhood* is an examination of the same ground covered in *The Godfather*. A comparison of Kirk Douglas' aging *capo* with Marlon Brando is embarrassing to the latter, though of course Brando didn't have much of a part to work with. Douglas does. Screenwriter Lewis John Carlino sets the conflict between two brothers, one the old boss hanging on to the old ways, the other, younger, giving up the closed Mafia for the ethnically open and structurally modern syndicate. This is no sentimental tale dissolving into a pseudo-moralistic blood-isthicker-than-water gumdrop; *The Brotherhood* is a lot tougher and more realistic than that. In lurid color appropriate to his story, Ritt paints a portrait of a man (played a little woodenly by Alex Cord, unfortunately) who must kill his older brother because he stands in the way of progress and profits. In every way—Carlino's tough script, Douglas' dynamic acting, Ritt's muscular direction, *The Broth-erhood* is the better picture. Coppola's pale colors aptly symbolize the way he has washed all power, all troubling energy out of his film.

Similarly, Corman's epic life of Ma Barker is proof of the kind of film that could have been made from the Benton-Newman screenplay. Again, as with Ritt, the most immediately striking difference is Corman's shocking use of color. But a more impor-

BLOODY MAMA (1970). With Clint Kimbrough, Shelley Winters, and extras

tant difference is the acting. Corman has dipped into the AIP repertory company and come up with a brilliant cast including Don Stroud, Pat Hingle, Diane Varsi, Bruce Dern, and Robert De Niro, all of them perfect in their roles. Corman doesn't shy away from the reality of the mad mama and her love for her moronic sons the way Penn does from his two losers. In fact, Corman elicits from Shelley Winters, as Mrs. Barker, one of the best performances of her career, a ruttish, lunatic tour-de-force. It is fascinating to speculate what Corman could have made, with Varsi, say, and Dern or De Niro, of *Bonnie and Clyde*. But then it probably would have attracted hardly any more attention than did *Bloody Mama*. Something like the slap in the face administered by a viewing of *Bonnie and Clyde* hits audiences of *Bloody Mama*. As the police and the cornered gang square off for the final gory shoot-out, carloads of sightseers arrive to watch the event. In that instant, Corman buries the hook, catching the audience on its own participation in the carnage that has gone before. Ritt, Corman, and Penn force the viewer to look at himself, to think about the ways in which, in a wider sense, he is implicated in the events of the society around him. Coppola's film, on the other hand, might just as well have been called *The Sound of Machine Guns*.

Artistic peaks tend to obscure the surrounding landscape, often seeming more important at first appearance than they really are. *Bonnie and Clyde* seemed like a cultural highwater mark, and yet only two years later Corman was able to equal Penn's achievement. *The Godfather* threatened to sink the gangster film under the gross weight of its pretensions, but less than two years later the gangster film is alive and well and living in Boston.

Boston is the setting for *The Friends of Eddie Coyle* (1973), Peter Yates' compelling version of George V. Higgins' novel about the life of a small-time hood. Robert Mitchum is Eddie Coyle, a weary, middle-aged soldier facing two-to-five on a rap in New Hampshire. For a living he supplies guns to a gang pulling bank holdups in the Boston suburbs. On the side, he is trying to parlay a little information into a parole up north: he is fifty years old, after all, with a wife and three kids to support.

Coyle is known as "Fingers" because his left hand was smashed in a drawer by friends of a client of his who was traced by the hot guns he supplied. He takes his "extra set of knuckles" in stride, like he takes everything. He is a long way from *Little Caesar*; Rico lived, Coyle survives.

Robert Mitchum is an actor —there have been others, Sterling Hayden, George Peppard, Robert Ryan—who has rarely had parts that fit. The combination of physical power and intellect is too strong for most roles, but in Eddie Coyle it all comes together. For one thing, Mitchum looks the part. The paunch, the pallor, the face that looks as if it has been slept in, the heavy walk capture perfectly

THE GANGSTER FILM TODAY

the seedy pathos of a 1970s Baby Face Nelson. Mitchum brings Coyle to life, giving him a tough dignity that makes him into a kind of working-class hero. Coyle is hard enough to finger his gun supplier for a lighter sentence, shrewd enough not to get caged by his police contact, and open enough to trust a friend who is his accuser and assassin. Mitchum plays Coyle's complexity for all its worth in a brilliant performance, one of the best of his career.

Yates is a skillful craftsman who assembles his elements unerringly and unobtrusively, building through careful attention to detail the kind of authority that was apparently intended for *The Godfather*. Paul Monash's script, following Higgins closely, is marvelously true to life. And the supporting cast, from Richard Jordan's sour cop through Steven Keats' edgy gun runner, is superlative. Peter Boyle is a study in quiet menace as the ex-con bartender who fingers Eddie and then kills him.

Eddie Coyle and his friends are not the only evidence of the continuing vitality of the gangster film. For example, the last several years have produced several black exploitation films that used gangster conventions effectively. A couple of years ago Hollywood decided to take account of the black-American audience. Spurred on by the financial success of a few prototypes, the movie business began after years of neglect to make motion pictures in great numbers with blacks in mind. Most of these pictures were trashy, exploiting anti-black clichés and the hostility of both parts of the audience with an eye on the buck. But in a few cases, filmmakers of talent set out to make real movies, and several of them succeeded.

One of the best was *Come*

THE FRIENDS OF EDDIE COYLE (1973). With Robert Mitchum and Peter Boyle

COME BACK, CHARLSTON BLUE (1972). With Godfrey Cambridge and Raymond St. Jacques

THE FRIENDS OF EDDIE COYLE (1973). The gang prepares to kidnap a bank manager.

SUPERFLY (1972). Ron O'Neal in the title role

Back, Charleston Blue (1972), second in a series featuring Coffin Ed Johnson and Gravedigger Jones, the Harlem police detectives invented by novelist Chester Himes. Given zestful readings by Raymond St. Jacques and Godfrey Cambridge, *Come Back, Charleston Blue* is a bittersweet look at ghetto life, given added punch by the skillful direction of Mark Warren, a television refugee (from "Laugh-In") from whom more should be seen. *Come Back, Charleston Blue* is a very different movie, faster and slicker than *Cotton Comes to Harlem*, which appeared a year earlier with the same cast under Ossie Davis' direction.

Financially, the most successful black film was *Superfly* (1972), about the troubles with the white mob of a black cocaine peddler. Featuring Ron O'Neal, the first star to emerge from the new black films, *Superfly* was most significant for what it revealed of the directing talents of Gordon Parks Jr., whose first film it was. Although his technique was crude, Parks gave the film a rambunctious pace and a visual style that was lost, unfortunately, under O'Neal's own direction of the sequel, *Superfly T.N.T.* (1973), a movie as disastrously weak as the first one was strong.

The most successful black series so far has belonged to Gordon Parks Sr. Although perhaps not the natural director that his son gives promise of being, the elder Parks has become much more assured as he has run Richard Roundtree through the first two of three films featuring the black private detective called John Shaft. These are the most conventional of the black cycle in their use of traditional material, even, for example, to having the major antagonist of the first chapter, *Shaft* (1971), based on a real life Harlem racketeer named Bumpy Jonas. Roundtree is a convincing Philip Marlowe in a black urban milieu, playing him with the same hard-boiled shrewdness of the best dicks of the past, and his assurance has grown with each screen appearance. The third, *Shaft in Africa* (1973), directed by John Guillermin, is arguably the best black film so far, though it is given a run for its money by Melvin Van Peebles' perverse, virtuoso *Sweet Sweetback's Badass Song* (1971), a thriller that used many of the conventions of the gangster film.

In addition, there continues

SHAFT (1971). Richard Roundtree as John Shaft

to be action from more traditional sources. While *The Godfather* was dominating the entertainment pages, another film, Terence Young's *The Valachi Papers* (1972) was attracting the attention of gangster cultists. Played by the brutish Charles Bronson as part of what will no doubt be a set of racketeer portrayals, Valachi came across intermittently with some of the punch missing from the bourgeois Corleones.

As this book went to press,

THE VALACHI PAPERS (1972). Charles Bronson as Joe Valachi

Honor Thy Father, Gay Talese's true-life study of a Mafia family, was just around the bend, soon to be followed by *Pretty Boy Floyd*, part of an announced series of screen biographies of noted criminals by American-International Pictures. All of which seems to indicate that there is a lot of life left in the old format.

By now we can see that the separation of movies into categories called genres offers us a tool with which to begin discriminating further among films. The existence of genre conventions is what allows us to see the shape of gangster film history, to see how filmmakers have solved the same problems differently or used the same material to express different realities, to record how values and attitudes have changed, to evaluate directors by understanding how one "transcends" genre limitations while another becomes bogged down in cliché. We are not taken in by *The Godfather's* pretensions and technical expertise because we have seen the same material handled more compellingly by other directors.

Until the day when cassettes make film history easily available to everyone, we will have to depend on convenient academic classifications like genre to advance our knowledge of film history. When we can all own inexpensive copies of the great and not-so-great films the way we can own classic and popular novels, when film appreciation becomes part of the standard liberal arts curriculum, then a film aesthetic will develop based on the quality of great films rather than on the careers of directors or their patterns of interest. Undoubtedly genre will remain an important critical concept and the achievements of directors will continue to be useful as they are in the study of literature and the arts and surely critics and textbook writers will discover stylistic "schools", but it is the individual film masterpieces that will remain the gold that must be dug out of the mine of cinema history.

THE GANGSTER FILM: A FILMOGRAPHY

The director's name follows the release date. A (c) *following the release date indicates that the film was in color. Sp indicates Screenplay and b/o indicates based/on.*

AL CAPONE. A John H. Burrows-Leonard J. Ackerman Production, released by Allied Artists, 1959. *Richard Wilson.* Sp: Malvin Wald and Henry Greenberg. Cast: Rod Steiger, Fay Spain, Murvyn Vye, James Gregory, Nehemiah Persoff.

ALIBI. Feature Productions, 1929. *Roland West.* Sp: Ronald West, C. Gardner Sullivan. Cast: Chester Morris, Regis Toomey, Pat O'Malley.

ANGELS WASH THEIR FACES. Warners, 1939. *Ray Enright.* Sp: Michael Fessier, Niven Busch, and Robert Buckner, b/o idea by Jonathan Finn. Cast: Ann Sheridan, Billy Halop, Bernard Punsley, Huntz Hall, Bobby Jordan, Leo Gorcey, Ronald Reagan.

ANGELS WITH DIRTY FACES. Warners, 1938. *Michael Curtiz.* Sp: John Wexley and Warren Duff, b/o play by Rowland Brown. Cast: James Cagney, Pat O'Brien, Ann Sheridan, the Dead End Kids.

THE ASPHALT JUNGLE. MGM, 1950. *John Huston.* Sp: Ben Maddow and John Huston, b/o novel by W. R. Burnett. Sp: Sterling Hayden, Louis Calhern, Sam Jaffe, Jean Hagen, James Whitmore, Marilyn Monroe.

BABY FACE NELSON. Fryman-ZS Films, released by United Artists, 1957. *Don Siegel.* Sp: Irving Shulman and Daniel Mainwaring, b/o story by Irving Shulman. Cast: Mickey Rooney, Carolyn Jones, Sir Cedric Hardwicke, Leo Gordon.

BEYOND A REASONABLE DOUBT. RKO, 1956. *Fritz Lang.* Sp: Douglas Morrow, b/o his story. Cast: Dana Andrews, Joan Fontaine, Sidney Blackmer, Philip Bourneuf.

THE BIG COMBO. A Security-Theodora Production, released by Allied Artists, 1955. *Joseph Lewis.* Sp: Philip Yordan. Cast: Cornel Wilde, Richard Conte, Jean Wallace, Brian Donlevy, Robert Middleton.

THE BIG SLEEP. Warners, 1946. *Howard Hawks*. Sp: William Faulkner and Leigh Brackett, b/o novel by Raymond Chandler. Cast: Humphrey Bogart, Lauren Bacall, Martha Vickers, Charles Waldron, John Ridgely, Elisha Cook Jr.

BLONDE CRAZY. Warners, 1931. *Roy Del Ruth*. Sp: Kubec Glasmon and John Bright. Cast: James Cagney, Joan Blondell, Louis Calhern, Ray Milland, Nat Pendleton.

BLONDIE JOHNSON. Warners, 1933. *Ray Enright*. Sp: Earl Baldwin, b/o his story. Cast: Joan Blondell, Chester Morris, Allen Jenkins, Claire Dodd, Mae Busch.

BLOODY MAMA. American International, 1970. (c) *Roger Corman*. Sp: Robert Thom and Don Peters. Cast: Shelley Winters, Don Stroud, Pat Hingle, Robert De Niro, Clint Kimbrough.

BONNIE AND CLYDE. Warner Bros.-Seven Arts, 1967. (c)*Arthur Penn*. Sp: David Newman and Robert Benton. Cast: Warren Beatty, Faye Dunaway, Gene Hackman, Michael Pollard, Estelle Parsons.

THE BONNIE PARKER STORY. American International, 1958. *William Witney*. Sp: Stanley Shpetner. Cast: Dorothy Provine, Jack Hogan, Richard Bakalyan, Joseph Turkel.

BOOMERANG. 20th Century-Fox, 1947. *Elia Kazan*. Sp: Richard Murphy, b/o article by Anthony Abbot. Cast: Dana Andrews, Arthur Kennedy, Jane Wyatt, Lee J. Cobb, Cara Williams.

BORDER INCIDENT. MGM, 1949. *Anthony Mann*. Sp: John C. Higgins, b/o story by John C. Higgins and George Zuckerman. Cast: George Murphy, Ricardo Montalban, Howard da Silva, James Mitchell, Arnold Moss.

THE BRASHER DOUBLOON. 20th Century-Fox, 1947. *John Brahm*. Sp: Leonard Praskins, b/o novel "The High Window" by Raymond Chandler. Cast: George Montgomery, Nancy Guild, Conrad Janis, Roy Roberts, Fritz Kortner.

BROTHER ORCHID. Warners, 1940. *Lloyd Bacon*. Sp: Earl Baldwin, b/o story by Richard Connell. Cast: Edward G. Robinson, Ann Sothern, Humphrey Bogart, Donald Crisp, Ralph Bellamy, Allen Jenkins.

THE BROTHERHOOD. Paramount, 1968. (c) *Martin Ritt*. Sp: Lewis John Carlino. Cast: Kirk Douglas, Alex Cord, Murray Hamilton, Luther Adler, Eduardo Ciannelli.

THE BROTHERS RICO. Columbia, 1957. *Phil Karlson*. Sp: Lewis Meltzer and Ben Perry, b/o novel by Georges Simenon. Cast: Richard Conte, Dianne Foster, Kathryn Grant, James Darren.

BRUTE FORCE. Universal-International, 1947. *Jules Dassin*. Sp: Richard Brooks, b/o story by Robert Patterson. Cast: Burt Lancaster, Hume Cronyn, Charles Bickford, Sam Levene, Howard Duff, Yvonne de Carlo, Ann Blyth, Ella Raines.

BULLETS OR BALLOTS. Warners, 1936. *William Keighley*. Sp: Seton T. Miller, b/o story by Martin Mooney and Seton I. Miller. Cast: Edward G. Robinson, Joan Blondell, Barton MacLane, Humphrey Bogart, Frank McHugh.

THE CASE AGAINST BROOKLYN. Columbia, 1958. *Paul Wendkos*. Sp: Raymond T. Marcus, b/o story by Daniel B. Ullman and article by Ed Reid. Cast: Darren McGavin, Maggie Hayes, Warren Stevens, Peggy McCay.

CITY STREETS. Paramount, 1931. *Rouben Mamoulian*. Sp: Oliver H.P. Garrett and Max Marcin, b/o story by Dashiell Hammett. Cast: Sylvia Sidney, Gary Cooper, Paul Lukas, William Boyd, Guy Kibbee, Stanley Fields, Wynne Gibson.

COME BACK, CHARLESTON BLUE. A Samuel Goldwyn Jr. Production, released by Warner Bros., 1972. (c) . *Mark Warren*. Sp: Bontche Schweig and Peggy Elliott, b/o "The Heat's On" by Chester Himes. Cast: Godfrey Cambridge, Raymond St. Jacques.

COOGAN'S BLUFF. Universal, 1968.(c) *Donald Siegel*. Sp: Herman Miller, Dean Riesner, and Howard Rodman, b/o story by Herman Miller. Cast: Clint Eastwood, Lee J. Cobb, Susan Clark, Betty Field, Tisha Sterling.

CRIME SCHOOL. Warners, 1938. *Lewis Seiler*. Sp: Crane Wilbur and Vincent Sherman, b/o story by Crane Wilbur. Cast: Humphrey Bogart, Gale Page, the Dead End Kids, George Offerman Jr., Cy Kendall.

CRIME WAVE (The City is Dark) Warners, 1954. *Andre de Toth*. Sp: Crane Wilbur, adapted by Bernard Gordon and Richard Wormser from story by John and Ward Hawkins. Cast: Gene Nelson, Sterling Hayden, Phyllis Kirk, Ted de Corsia.

THE CRIMSON KIMONO. Columbia, 1959. *Samuel Fuller*. Sp: Samuel Fuller. Cast: Glenn Corbett, Victoria Shaw, James Shigeta, Anna Lee.

CRISS CROSS. Universal-International, 1949. *Robert Siodmak*. Sp: Daniel Fuchs, b/o novel by Don Tracy. Cast: Burt Lancaster, Yvonne de Carlo, Dan Duryea, Stephen McNally, Richard Long, Tom Pedi.

CRY OF THE CITY. 20th Century-Fox, 1948. *Robert Siodmak*. Sp: Richard Murphy, b/o novel "The Chair for Martin Rome," by Henry Edward Helseth. Cast: Victor Mature, Richard Conte, Shelley Winters, Fred Clark, Hope Emerson.

D.O.A. A Harry M. Popkin Production, released by United Artists, 1950. *Rudolph Maté*. Sp: Russell Rouse and Clarence Greene. Cast: Edmond O'Brien, Pamela Britton, Luther Adler, Beverly Campbell, Lynn Baggett.

DARK CITY. Paramount, 1950. *William Dieterle*. Sp: John Meredyth Lucas and Larry Marcus, adapted by Ketti Frings from story by Larry Marcus. Cast: Charlton Heston, Lizabeth Scott, Viveca Lindfors, Dean Jagger, Jack Webb, Don DeFore.

THE DARK CORNER. 20th Century-Fox, 1946. *Henry Hathaway*. Sp: Jay Dratler and Bernard Schoenfeld, b/o story by Leo Rosten. Cast: Lucille Ball, Mark Stevens, Clifton Webb, William Bendix, Kurt Kreuger, Cathy Downs.

DARK PASSAGE. Warners, 1947. *Delmer Daves*. Sp: Delmer Daves, b/o novel by David Goodis. Cast: Humphrey Bogart, Lauren Bacall, Agnes Moorehead, Bruce Bennett, Tom D'Andrea.

DEAD END. A Samuel Goldwyn Production, released by United Artists, 1937. *William Wyler*. Sp: Lillian Hellman, b/o play by Sidney Kingsley. Cast: Joel McCrea, Sylvia Sidney, Humphrey Bogart, Wendy Barrie, Claire Trevor, Allen Jenkins, Marjorie Main, Billy Halop, Leo Gorcey.

DILLINGER. Monogram, 1945. *Max Nosseck*. Sp: Philip Yordan. Cast: Lawrence Tierney, Edmund Lowe, Anne Jeffreys, Eduardo Ciannelli, Marc Lawrence, Elisha Cook Jr.

DILLINGER. American International, 1973. *John Milius*. Sp: John Milius. Cast: Warren Oates, Ben Johnson, Cloris Leachman, Michelle Phillips.

THE DOORWAY TO HELL. Warners, 1930. *Archie Mayo*. Sp: Rowland Brown. Cast: Lew Ayres, Charles Judels, Dorothy Mathews, James Cagney, Leon Janney.

DOUBLE INDEMNITY. Paramount, 1944. *Billy Wilder*. Sp: Billy Wilder and Raymond Chandler, b/o novel by James M. Cain. Cast: Barbara Stanwyck, Fred MacMurray, Edward G. Robinson, Porter Hall, Jean Heather, Tom Powers.

DOWN THREE DARK STREETS. An Edward Small Production, released by United Artists, 1954. *Arnold Laven*. Sp: Gordon and Mildred Gordon and

Bernard C. Schoenfeld. Cast: Broderick Crawford, Ruth Roman, Martha Hyer, Marissa Pavan, Casey Adams.

THE ENFORCER. Warners, 1951. *Bretaigne Windust.* Sp: Martin Rackin. Cast: Humphrey Bogart, Zero Mostel, Ted De Corsia, Everett Sloane, Roy Roberts.

FIVE AGAINST THE HOUSE. Columbia, 1955. *Phil Karlson.* Sp: Stirling Silliphant, William Bowers, and John Barnwell, b/o story by Jack Finney. Cast: Guy Madison, Kim Novak, Brian Keith, Alvy Moore, Kerwin Mathews.

FORCE OF EVIL. Enterprise, 1948. *Abraham Polonsky.* Sp: Abraham Polonsky and Ira Wolfert, b/o novel "Tucker's People" by Ira Wolfert. Cast: John Garfield, Beatrice Pearson, Thomas Gomez, Roy Roberts, Marie Windsor.

THE FRENCH CONNECTION. 20th Century-Fox, 1972. (c) . *William Friedkin.* Sp: Ernest Tidyman, b/o novel by Robin Moore. Cast: Gene Hackman, Fernando Rey, Roy Scheider, Tony Lo Bianco, Marcel Bozzuffi.

THE FRIENDS OF EDDIE COYLE. Paramount, 1973. (c) . *Peter Yates.* Sp: Paul Monash, b/o novel by George V. Higgins. Cast: Robert Mitchum, Peter Boyle, Helena Carroll, Richard Jordan, Steven Keats.

G-MEN. Warners, 1935. *William Keighley.* Sp: Seton I. Miller, b/o story by Gregory Rogers. Cast: James Cagney, Margaret Lindsay, Ann Dvorak, Robert Armstrong, Barton MacLane, Lloyd Nolan.

THE GANGSTER. Allied Artists, 1947. *Gordon Wiles.* Sp: Daniel Fuchs, b/o his novel "Low Company." Cast: Barry Sullivan, Belita, Joan Lorring, Akim Tamiroff, John Ireland, Henry Morgan.

THE GARMENT JUNGLE. Columbia, 1957. *Vincent Sherman* (reputedly directed largely by *Robert Aldrich*). Sp: Harry Kleiner, b/o articles by Lester Velie. Cast: Lee J. Cobb, Kerwin Mathews, Gia Scala, Richard Boone, Robert Loggia.

THE GEORGE RAFT STORY. Allied Artists, 1961. *Joseph M. Newman.* Sp: Crane Wilbur. Cast: Ray Danton, Jayne Mansfield, Julie London, Barrie Chase, Herschel Bernardi, Frank Gorshin.

GET CARTER. MGM, 1971. (c) *Michael Hodges.* Sp: Michael Hodges, based on novel "Jack's Return Home" by Ted Lewis. Cast: Michael Caine, Ian Hendry, Britt Eklund, John Osborne.

THE GLASS KEY. Paramount, 1942. *Stuart Heisler.* Sp: Jonathan Latimer, b/o novel by Dashiell Hammett. Cast: Brian Donlevy, Alan Ladd, Veronica Lake, Bonita Granville, William Bendix, Joseph Calleia.

THE GODFATHER. Paramount, 1972. (c) *Francis Ford Coppola*. Sp: Francis Ford Coppola and Mario Puzo, b/o novel by Mario Puzo. Cast: Marlon Brando, Al Pacino, James Caan, Robert Duvall, Richard Castellano, Diane Keaton.

GUMSHOE. Columbia, 1971. *Stephen Frears*. Sp: Neville Smith. Cast: Albert Finney, Billie Whitelaw, Frank Finlay, Janice Rule.

GUN CRAZY. A King Production, released by United Artists, 1950. *Joseph H. Lewis*. Sp: MacKinlay Kantor and Millard Kaufman, b/o story by MacKinlay Kantor. Cast: John Dall, Peggy Cummins, Barry Kroeger, Annabel Shaw, Morris Carnovsky.

GUNN. Paramount, 1967. (c) *Blake Edwards*. Sp: Blake Edwards and William Peter Blatty, b/o characters created by Edwards. Cast: Craig Stevens, Laura Devon, Edward Asner, Albert Paulsen, Helen Traubel.

HARPER. Warners, 1966. (c) *Jack Smight*. Sp: William Goldman, b/o novel "The Moving Target" by Ross MacDonald. Cast: Paul Newman, Lauren Bacall, Julie Harris, Arthur Hill, Janet Leigh, Pamela Tiffin, Robert Wagner.

THE HATCHET MAN. Warners, 1932. *William A. Wellman*. Sp: J. Grubb Alexander, b/o play by Achmed Abdullah and David Belasco. Cast: Edward G. Robinson, Loretta Young, Dudley Digges, J. Carroll Naish, Blanche Frederici.

HIGH SIERRA. Warners, 1941. *Raoul Walsh*. Sp: John Huston and W. R. Burnett, b/o novel by W. R. Burnett. Cast: Humphrey Bogart, Ida Lupino, Alan Curtis, Arthur Kennedy, Joan Leslie, Henry Hull, Henry Travers.

HOUSE OF BAMBOO. 20th Century-Fox, 1955. (c) *Samuel Fuller*. Sp: Harry Kleiner. Cast: Robert Ryan, Robert Stack, Shirley Yamaguchi, Cameron Mitchell, Brad Dexter, Sessue Hayakawa.

THE HOUSE ON NINETY-SECOND STREET. 20th Century-Fox, 1945. *Henry Hathaway*. Sp: Charles G. Booth, Barre Lyndon, and John Monks Jr., b/o story by Charles G. Booth taken from cases in FBI files. Cast: William Eythe, Lloyd Nolan, Signe Hasso, Gene Lockhart, Leo G. Carroll, Lydia St. Clair.

I AM THE LAW. Columbia, 1938. *Alexander Hall*. Sp: Jo Swerling, b/o stories by Fred Allhoff. Cast: Edward G. Robinson, Barbara O'Neil, John Beal, Wendy Barrie, Otto Kruger.

I DIED A THOUSAND TIMES. Warners, 1955. *Stuart Heisler*. Sp: W. R. Burnett, b/o his novel "High Sierra." Cast: Jack Palance, Shelley Winters,

Lori Nelson, Lon Chaney, Earl Holliman. Remake of *High Sierra* (1941).

I WALK ALONE. Paramount, 1948. *Byron Haskin*. Sp: Charles Schnee, adapted by Robert Smith and John Bright from play "Beggars are Coming to Town" by Theodore Reeves. Cast: Burt Lancaster, Lizabeth Scott, Kirk Douglas, Wendell Corey, Kristine Miller.

IT ALL CAME TRUE. Warners, 1940. *Lewis Seiler*. Sp: Michael Fessier and Lawrence Kimble, b/o novelette "And It All Came True" by Louis Bromfield. Cast: Ann Sheridan, Humphrey Bogart, Jeffrey Lynn, ZaSu Pitts, Una O'Connor.

KANSAS CITY CONFIDENTIAL. An Edward Small production released by United Artists, 1952. Sp: George Bruce and Harry Essex, b/o story by Harold Greene and Rowland Brown. Cast: John Payne, Coleen Gray, Preston Foster, Lee Van Cleef, Neville Brand.

KEY LARGO. Warners, 1948. *John Huston*. Sp: Richard Brooks and John Huston, b/o play by Maxwell Anderson. Cast: Humphrey Bogart, Edward G. Robinson, Lauren Bacall, Lionel Barrymore, Claire Trevor, Thomas Gomez.

THE KILLERS. Universal, 1946. *Robert Siodmak*. Sp: Anthony Veiller, b/o story by Ernest Hemingway. Cast: Burt Lancaster, Ava Gardner, Edmond O'Brien, Albert Dekker, Sam Levene.

THE KILLERS. Universal, 1964. (c) *Don Siegel*. Sp: Gene L. Coon, b/o story by Ernest Hemingway. Cast: Lee Marvin, Angie Dickinson, John Cassavetes, Ronald Reagan, Clu Gulager.

KISS ME DEADLY. A Parklane Production, released by United Artists, 1955. *Robert Aldrich*. Sp: A. I. Bezzerides, b/o novel by Mickey Spillane. Cast: Ralph Meeker, Albert Dekker, Cloris Leachman, Paul Stewart, Juano Hernandez.

KISS OF DEATH. 20th Century-Fox, 1947. *Henry Hathaway*. Sp: Ben Hecht and Charles Lederer, b/o story by Eleazar Lipsky. Cast: Victor Mature, Richard Widmark, Brian Donlevy, Coleen Gray, Karl Malden, Taylor Holmes.

KISS TOMORROW GOODBYE. Warners, 1950. *Gordon Douglas*. Sp: Harry Brown, b/o novel by Horace McCoy. Cast: James Cagney, Barbara Payton, Ward Bond, Luther Adler, Barton MacLane, Helena Carter.

LADY IN THE LAKE. MGM, 1947. *Robert Montgomery*. Sp: Steve Fisher, b/o novel by Raymond Chandler. Cast: Robert Montgomery, Audrey Totter, Lloyd Nolan, Tom Tully, Leon Ames, Jayne Meadows.

LADY SCARFACE. RKO, 1941. *Frank Woodruff*. Sp: Arnaud D'Usseau and Richard Collins. Cast: Judith Anderson, Dennis O'Keefe, Frances Neal, Eric Blore, Marc Lawrence.

LITTLE CAESAR. Warners, 1930. *Mervyn LeRoy*. Sp: Francis Edwards Faragoh, b/o novel by W. R. Burnett. Cast: Edward G. Robinson, Glenda Farrell, Douglas Fairbanks Jr., George E. Stone, Sidney Blackmer.

MACHINE GUN KELLY. Anglo Amalgamated, 1958. *Roger Corman*. Sp: R. Wright Campbell. Cast: Charles Bronson, Susan Cabot, Morey Amsterdam, Wally Campo.

MADIGAN. Universal, 1968. (c) *Don Siegel*. Sp: Henri Simoun and Abraham Polonsky, b/o novel "The Commissioner" by Richard Dougherty. Cast: Richard Widmark, Henry Fonda, Inger Stevens, Harry Guardino, James Whitmore, Susan Clark.

THE MALTESE FALCON. Warners, 1941. *John Huston*. Sp: John Huston, b/o novel by Dashiell Hammett. Cast: Humphrey Bogart, Mary Astor, Sydney Greenstreet, Peter Lorre, Elisha Cook Jr., Lee Patrick, Jerome Cowan.

MARLOWE. MGM, 1969. (c) *Paul Bogart*. Sp: Stirling Silliphant, b/o novel "The Little Sister" by Raymond Chandler. Cast: James Garner, Gayle Hunnicut, Rita Moreno, Carroll O'Connor.

MURDER BY CONTRACT. Columbia, 1958. *Irving Lerner*. Sp: Ben Simcoe b/o his story. Cast: Vince Edwards, Philip Pine, Herschel Bernardi, Caprice Toriel.

MURDER, INC. 20th Century-Fox, 1960. *Stuart Rosenberg and Burt Balaban*. Sp: Irve Tunick and Mel Barr, b/o book by Burton Turkus and Sid Feder. Cast: Stuart Whitman, May Britt, Peter Falk, Henry Morgan, David J. Stewart.

MURDER, MY SWEET. RKO, 1945. *Edward Dmytryk*. Sp: John Paxton, b/o novel "Farewell, My Lovely" by Raymond Chandler. Cast: Dick Powell, Claire Trevor, Anne Shirley, Otto Kruger, Mike Mazurki.

MYSTERY STREET. MGM, 1950. *John Sturges*. Sp: Sydney Boehm and Richard Brooks, b/o story by Leonard Spigelgass. Cast: Ricardo Montalban, Sally Forrest. Bruce Bennett, Elsa Lanchester, Jan Sterling, Marshall Thompson.

THE NAKED CITY. Universal-International, 1948. *Jules Dassin*. Sp: Albert Maltz and Malvin Wald, b/o story by Malvin Wald. Cast: Barry Fitzgerald, Howard Duff, Dorothy Hart, Don Taylor, Ted De Corsia.

NIGHT AND THE CITY. 20th Century-Fox, 1950. *Jules Dassin*. Sp: Jo Eisinger, b/o novel by Gerald Kersh. Cast: Richard Widmark, Gene Tierney, Googie Withers, Hugh Marlowe, Francis L. Sullivan.

ON DANGEROUS GROUND. RKO, 1952. *Nicholas Ray*. Sp: A.I. Bezzerides, b/o novel "Mad With Much Heart" by Gerald Butler. Cast: Robert Ryan, Ida Lupino, Ward Bond, Charles Kemper, Anthony Ross, Ed Begley.

ON THE WATERFRONT. Columbia, 1954. *Elia Kazan*. Sp: Budd Schulberg, b/o story by Budd Schulberg and articles by Malcolm Johnson. Cast: Marlon Brando, Eva Marie Saint, Lee J. Cobb, Rod Steiger, Karl Malden, Pat Henning.

OUT OF THE PAST. RKO, 1947. *Jacques Tourneur*. Sp: Geoffrey Homes. Cast: Robert Mitchum, Kirk Douglas, Jane Greer, Rhonda Fleming, Richard Webb.

PANIC IN THE STREETS. 20th Century-Fox, 1950. *Elia Kazan*. Sp: Richard Murphy, adapted by Daniel Fuchs from story by Edna and Edward Anhalt. Cast: Richard Widmark, Paul Douglas, Barbara Bel Geddes, Walter (Jack) Palance, Zero Mostel.

PARTY GIRL. MGM, 1958. *Nicholas Ray*. Sp: George Wells, b/o story by Leo Katcher. Cast: Robert Taylor, Cyd Charisse, Lee J. Cobb, John Ireland, Kent Smith, Claire Kelly.

PAY OR DIE. Allied Artists, 1960. *Richard Wilson*. Sp: Richard Collins and Bertram Millhauser. Cast: Ernest Borgnine, Zohra Lampert, Alan Austin, Renata Vanni, Bruno Della Santina.

THE PHENIX CITY STORY. Allied Artists, 1955. *Phil Karlson*. Sp: Crane Wilbur and Dan Mainwaring. Cast: John McIntire, Richard Kiley, Kathryn Grant, Edward Andrews, James Edwards.

PICKUP ON SOUTH STREET. 20th Century-Fox, 1953. *Samuel Fuller*. Sp: Samuel Fuller, b/o story by Dwight Taylor. Cast: Richard Widmark, Jean Peters, Thelma Ritter, Murvyn Vye, Richard Kiley.

POINT BLANK. MGM, 1967 (c) *John Boorman*. Sp: Alexander Jacobs and David and Rafe Newhouse, b/o novel "The Hunter" by Richard Stark. Cast: Lee Marvin, Angie Dickinson, Keenan Wynn, Carroll O'Connor, Lloyd Bochner, Michael Strong.

PORTRAIT OF A MOBSTER. Warners, 1961. *Joseph Pevney*. Sp: Howard Browne, b/o book by Harry Grey. Cast: Vic Morrow, Leslie Parrish, Peter Breck, Ray Danton.

THE PUBLIC ENEMY . Warners, 1931. *William A. Wellman*. Sp: Harvey Thew, b/o story by Kubec Glasmon and John Bright. Cast: James Cagney, Edward Woods, Jean Harlow, Donald Cook, Joan Blondell, Beryl Mercer.

PUBLIC ENEMY'S WIFE. Warners, 1936. *Nick Grinde*. Sp: Abem Finkel and Harold Buckley, b/o story by P. J. Wolfson. Cast: Margaret Lindsay, Pat O'Brien, Robert Armstrong, Cesar Romero, Dick Foran.

PUBLIC HERO NO. 1. MGM, 1935. *J. Walter Ruben*. Sp: Wells Root, b/o story by J. Walter Ruben and Wells Root. Cast: Lionel Barrymore, Jean Arthur, Chester Morris, Joseph Calleia, Paul Kelly, Lewis Stone.

PULP. A Klinger-Caine Hodges Production, released by United Artists, 1972. *Michael Hodges*. Sp: Michael Hodges. Cast: Michael Caine, Mickey Rooney Lizabeth Scott, Lionel Stander.

RACKET BUSTERS. Warners, 1938. *Lloyd Bacon*. Sp: Robert Rossen and Leonardo Bercovici. Cast: Humphrey Bogart, George Brent, Gloria Dickson, Allen Jenkins, Walter Abel.

RAW DEAL. A Reliance Picture released by Eagle-Lion, 1948. *Anthony Mann*. Sp: Leopold Atlas and John C. Higgins, b/o story by Arnold B. Armstrong and Audrey Ashley. Cast: Dennis O'Keefe, Claire Trevor, Marsha Hunt, John Ireland, Raymond Burr.

RIFIFI. United Motion Picture Organization, 1956. *Jules Dassin*. Sp: Jules Dassin, Rene Wheeler, and August le Breton, b/o novel by August le Breton. Cast: Jean Servais, Carl Mohner, Robert Manuel, Perlo Vita, (Jules Dassin), Marie Sabouret.

THE RISE AND FALL OF LEGS DIAMOND. Warners, 1960. *Budd Boetticher*. Sp: Joseph Landon. Cast: Ray Danton, Karen Steele, Elaine Stewart, Robert Lowery, Jesse White, Simon Oakland.

THE ROARING TWENTIES. Warners, 1939. *Raoul Walsh*. Sp: Jerry Wald, Richard Macaulay and Robert Rossen, b/o story by Mark Hellinger. Cast: James Cagney, Humphrey Bogart, Priscilla Lane, Gladys George, Jeffrey Lynn, Frank McHugh.

SCARFACE. A Howard Hughes Production, released by United Artists, 1932. *Howard Hawks*. Sp: Ben Hecht, b/o book by Armitage Trail. Cast: Paul Muni, Ann Dvorak, Karen Morley, Osgood Perkins, Boris Karloff, George Raft.

THE SCARFACE MOB. Desilu, 1962. *Phil Karlson*. Sp: Paul Monash, b/o novel "The Untouchables" by Eliot Ness and Oscar Fraley. Cast: Robert Stack, Keenan Wynn, Barbara Nichols, Pat Crowley, Neville Brand.

THE SECRET SIX. MGM, 1931. *George Hill*. Sp: Frances Marion, b/o her story. Cast: Clark Gable, Wallace Beery, Lewis Stone, John Mack Brown, Ralph Bellamy.

SHAFT. MGM, 1971. (c) *Gordon Parks*. Sp: Ernest Tidyman and John D. F. Black, b/o novel by Ernest Tidyman. Cast: Richard Roundtree, Moses Gunn, Charles Cioffi, Gwenn Mitchell, Christopher St. John.

SHAFT IN AFRICA. MGM, 1973. (c) *John Guillermin*. Sp: Stirling Silliphant. Cast: Richard Roundtree, Frank Finlay, Vonetta McGee, Neda Arneric.

SHAFT'S BIG SCORE. MGM, 1972. (c) *Gordon Parks*. Sp: Ernest Tidyman. Cast: Richard Roundtree, Kathy Imrie, Moses Gunn, Drew Bundini Brown.

SHAMUS. Columbia, 1973. (c) *Buzz Kulik*. Sp: Barry Beckerman. Cast: Burt Reynolds, Dyan Cannon, John Ryan, Joe Santos, Georgio Tozzi.

SIDE STREET. MGM, 1950. *Anthony Mann*. Sp: Sydney Boehm, b/o his story. Cast: Farley Granger, Cathy O'Donnell, James Craig, Paul Kelly, Jean Hagen.

THE SILENCERS. Columbia, 1966. (c) *Phil Karlson*. Sp: Oscar Saul, b/o books "The Silencers" and "Death of a Citizen" by Donald Hamilton. Cast: Dean Martin, Stella Stevens, Daliah Lavi, Victor Buono, Arthur O'Connell, Robert Webber.

SIX BRIDGES TO CROSS. Universal-International, 1955. *Joseph Pevney*. Sp: Sydney Boehm, b/o story by Joseph F. Dinneen. Cast: Tony Curtis, George Nader, Julie Adams, Sal Mineo, Jay C. Flippen.

SLAUGHTER ON TENTH AVENUE. Universal, 1957. *Arnold Laven*. Sp: Lawrence Roman, b/o book "The Man Who Rocked the Boat" by William J. Keating and Richard Carter. Cast: Richard Egan, Jan Sterling, Dan Duryea, Julie Adams, Walter Matthau, Sam Levene.

A SLIGHT CASE OF MURDER. Warners, 1938. *Lloyd Bacon*. Sp: Earl Baldwin and Joseph Schrank, b/o play by Damon Runyon and Howard Lindsay. Cast: Edward G. Robinson, Ruth Donnelly, Jane Bryan, Allen Jenkins, Willard Parker, John Litel.

THE ST. VALENTINE'S DAY MASSACRE. 20th Century-Fox, 1967. (c)

Roger Corman. Sp: Howard Browne. Cast: Jason Robards Jr., George Segal, Jean Hale, Ralph Meeker, Frank Silvera, Clint Ritchie.

THE STREET WITH NO NAME. 20th Century-Fox, 1948. *William Keighley*. Sp: Harry Kleiner. Cast: Mark Stevens, Richard Widmark, Lloyd Nolan, Barbara Lawrence, Ed Begley, Donald Buka.

SUPERFLY. Warners, 1972. (c) *Gordon Parks, Jr.* Sp: Philip Fenty. Cast: Ron O'Neal, Carl Lee, Sheila Frazier, Julius W. Harris.

T-MEN. Eagle-Lion, 1947. *Anthony Mann*. Sp: John C. Higgins, b/o story by Virginia Kellogg. Cast: Dennis O'Keefe, Mary Meade, Alfred Ryder, Wallace Ford, June Lockhart.

THEY LIVE BY NIGHT. RKO, 1949. *Nicholas Ray*. Sp: Charles Schnee, b/o novel "Thieves Like Us" by Edward Anderson. Cast: Cathy O'Donnell, Farley Granger, Howard da Silva, Jay C. Flippen.

THIS GUN FOR HIRE. Paramount, 1942. *Frank Tuttle*. Sp: Albert Maltz and W. R. Burnett, b/o novel by Graham Greene. Cast: Veronica Lake, Robert Preston, Laird Cregar, Alan Ladd, Tully Marshall, Mikhail Rasumny.

TIP-OFF GIRLS. Paramount, 1938. *Louis King*. Sp: Maxwell Shane, Stuart Yost, and Stuart Anthony. Cast: Lloyd Nolan, Mary Carlisle, Larry Crabbe, Roscoe Karns, Anthony Quinn.

TONY ROME. 20th Century-Fox, 1967. (c) *Gordon Douglas*. Sp: Richard Breen, b/o novel by Marvin H. Albert. Cast: Frank Sinatra, Jill St. John, Richard Conte, Gena Rowlands, Simon Oakland, Jeffrey Lynn, Sue Lyon.

THE UNDERCOVER MAN. Columbia, 1949. *Joseph H. Lewis*. Sp: Sydney Boehm, b/o Jack Rubin adaptation of article by Frank J. Wilson. Cast: Glenn Ford, Nina Foch, James Whitmore, Barry Kelley, David Wolfe.

UNDERWORLD. Paramount Famous Lasky Corp., 1927. *Josef von Sternberg*. Sp: Robert N. Lee. Titles: George Marion Jr. Adaptation: Charles Furthman. Story: Ben Hecht. Cast: George Bancroft, Clive Brook, Evelyn Brent, Larry Semon.

BIBLIOGRAPHY

Alloway, Lawrence. *Violent America: The Movies 1946-1964*. New York: The Museum of Modern Art, 1971.

Barbour, Alan G. *Humphrey Bogart*. New York: Pyramid Publications, 1973.

Baxter, John. *The Gangster Film*. New York: A.S. Barnes & Co., 1970.

Bergman, Andrew. *We're in the Money*. New York: Harper and Row, 1972.

Hecht, Ben, *A Child of the Century*. New York: Ballantine Book, 1970.

Kael, Pauline. *Kiss Kiss Bang Bang*. New York: Bantam Books, 1969.

MacDonald, Dwight. *On Movies*. New York: Berkley Medallion Books, 1971.

McArthur, Colin. *Underworld USA*. New York: The Viking Press, 1972.

Sacks, Arthur. "Gangster Movies of the Early Thirties." *The Velvet Light Trap*, No. 1, 1971. Madison, Wisconsin.

Sarris, Andrew. *The American Cinema*. New York: E.P. Dutton & Co., 1968.

Sarris, Andrew. *Confessions of a Cultist*. New York: Simon and Schuster, 1971.

Warshow, Robert. *The Immediate Experience*. New York: Atheneum, 1970.

INDEX

154

156

ABOUT THE AUTHOR

A writer and editor, John Gabree is the author of *Surviving the City* (Ballantine, 1973) and *The World of Rock* (Fawcett, 1968). He has reviewed films for *Fusion* magazine and other periodicals.

ABOUT THE EDITOR

Ted Sennett has been attending and enjoying movies since the age of two. He has written about films for magazines and newspapers, and is the author of WARNER BROTHERS PRESENTS, a survey of the great Warners films of the thirties and forties. A publishing executive, he lives in New Jersey with his wife and three children.